DISCIPLINE IN THE WILDERNESS

Challenges & Triumphs of a New Season

SHERIE M. DAVIS

Copyright © 2022 Sherie M. Davis

ALL RIGHTS RESERVED. This book contains material protected under International and Federal Copyright Laws and Treaties. Any unauthorized reprint or use of this material is prohibited. No part of this book may be reproduced or transmitted in any form or by any means, electronic or mechanical, including photocopying, recording, or by any information storage and retrieval system without express written permission from the author/publisher.

Scripture is taken from the New King James Version®. Copyright © 1982 by Thomas Nelson. All rights reserved.

All Scripture quotations, unless otherwise indicated, are taken from the Holy Bible, New International Version®, NIV®. Copyright ©1973, 1978, 1984, 2011 by Biblica, Inc.™ Used by permission of Zondervan. All rights reserved worldwide. www.zondervan.com The "NIV" and "New International Version" are trademarks registered in the United States Patent and Trademark Office by Biblica, Inc.™

Book Cover Design: Prize Publishing House

Printed by: Prize Publishing House, LLC in the United States of America.

First printing edition 2022.

Prize Publishing House
P.O. Box 9856, Chesapeake, VA 23321
www.PrizePublishingHouse.com

ISBN (Hardcover): 979-8-9858926-3-5
ISBN (E-Book): 979-8-9858926-4-2

Library of Congress Control Number: 2022906389

To my sister, Keshia, and my daughters, Tatyana & Tashanna, thank you for being such amazing sounding boards.

CONTENTS

Introduction vii

Chapter 1   When God Interrupts Your Normal 1
Chapter 2   The Wilderness' Purpose 17
Chapter 3   For the Making 24
Chapter 4   The Danger of Complacency 36
Chapter 5   No Other Gods 48
Chapter 6   Discipline the Flesh 57
Chapter 7   Progress Over Perfection 68
Chapter 8   Reset 77
Chapter 9   Praying & Fasting are Essential to a Wilderness 94
Chapter 10 The Red Sea 108

Conclusion 123
References 127

INTRODUCTION

Let me start by saying this; I am not a writer nor a public speaker. I just have something to say. I do not portray to have all the answers to every wilderness season, but I can certainly bear witness to God's power and patience in my own experience. This is not a quick read, and I encourage every reader to ponder while reading. Look within and use the Holy Bible to follow along with the references. I pray your understanding is enlightened by what is written here.

MIND MAINTENANCE AND MANAGEMENT

Discipline is psychological. It is a state of mind that must be trained to think or be a certain way. It is simply a decision we make every day about how to live, think, and go about life. Your actions are a choice of what you will focus on, and your life will directly reflect those choices. It all boils down to making the same decision consistently for the best outcome in life. Discipline can come through teaching from a mentor, self-discipline, or being trained by the Holy Ghost. It is an attribute that we need in life to keep us on a specific path, mostly God's divine path of life. We all need willpower and courage to maintain and manage our thoughts daily. People struggle with this reality because our thought life plays the most tricks on us. My former bishop, the Late Dr. Walter Leigh Bates, would always say, "Stop rewinding the tape in our heads." We rehearse failures, past traumas, and disappointments to the point we feel we are still there. This is usually a sign of clutter in the mind, and it is always best to declutter the subconscious part of our brain to clean out what lies beneath our consciousness. If that part of the mind remains cluttered, it is difficult to function in life and see-through clear lenses. Everything you see, you will always see a negative side as the subconscious can dictate your view of the world around you. Whatever is in there will show up in your life today and manifest similar hurt and pain from your past. You will know when your subconscious is cluttered. Here are the signs.

- Always on the defense of a matter
- Unforgiving
- Overly critical of yourself (self-loathing)
- Competitive with others
- Excessiveness (idolatry, overcompensating)
- Very manipulative
- Always dissatisfied
- Prideful
- Plays the victim
- Denial (hard to confront realities or truths)
- Fear to self-reflect or self-examine (avoidance)
- Attention seeker (by any means)
- Argumentative
- Battles with depression regularly
- Pessimistic about everything (seeing or believing the worse out of outcomes, hopelessness)
- Gossipy (lives to spill the tea)
- Jealous hearted

If your life possesses any of these characteristics, your subconscious may be cluttered with decades of pain, hurt, and disappointments. You have been replaying past adversity in your head, causing these characters to show up in your life today. It is time to declutter (mind maintenance). It is time to clean out what has been beneath the surface of your soul and impeding a distorted view of life. There are ways you can declutter. What helped me was daily confessions/reflections through journaling, and sometimes I confided in a trusted person. Therapy is another way of discovering the clutter in the subconscious. Considering any these, keep in mind that the decluttering process will require you to be humble and transparent, open and willing to tell the ugly truth about yourself. We cover up our wounds as we are afraid to be looked at differently or avoid the feeling of being weak, but we must understand that a wound covered up cannot be healed. The bandage of pride must be removed from the wound to be healed completely. Once the subconscious is clean, now it is time to replace all that clutter with the promises of God. This is when you begin to manage the mind by fasting. Study the Word of God more, pray more, forgive more, love more, cry a river, build a bridge, and get over it. The reality is that you are now in control, and you have what it takes to turn it all around for your good.

One of our psychological structure's hardest and lengthiest tasks is to be unprogrammed from old patterns. It is so hard to give up old natures and practices because we have used them to get by for so long, and it helps make sense of them. Once the mind is programmed to a specific structure or belief, it easily becomes settled and closed to new possibilities and realities. We can discipline the mind to learn as much as we will allow it to learn in whatever length of time. The meaning of discipline is to possess training or to bring to a state of order and obedience by training and control and to have improved skills which means to be disciplined, one must come into a willingness to be taught a new way of life. To reach high-level learning, the mind must be open and willing to learn when an opportunity arises.

We live in a world with such a cultural hype for food. Every culture comes with special cuisine, and these cuisines have become a part of the tradition, and it is forbidden to leave that tradition. It does not matter the negative effect these cuisines can inflict on your health; turning down cultural delicacies will sometimes get you frowned upon. I collaborated with an African American single mom in the community who is a certified chef. I can tell cooking was a form of therapy for her because when she spoke of creating through cooking, her face just lit up. Her favorite dishes were the traditional Black family cuisines (soul food). I mistakenly told her that I did not eat soul food, and as her face frowned, she asked, "Why?" I told her that I had decided for my life to do things a little differently. Well, that was not good enough for her. She had a puzzled look on her face. So, I said, "Besides, much of what we eat in the Black community is not healthy for us, and we're dying too soon." She stated, "Yeah, but our ancestors ate this way, and they proved that we could make something out of nothing." My response to her was very subtle as I did not want to offend her but to offer her a unique way of looking at the matter. I replied, "I respect our ancestors for surviving during the worse times of their lives, and I will always remember them for that, but that does not mean we have to eat the same way they did. Especially considering we are not in the situation they were in. We are free and have been given access to more, and I think they would be proud of us to pursue more." She did not have too much to say after that. Tradition can sometimes blind us from seeing new opportunities or when a new season is upon us. Anytime we enter a new season, a new mindset is required to get the best out of the season.

 As I get older, I realize I need to start eating healthier and developing a workout routine. The more I worked out, the more I realized that working out alters the mood and causes a more positive thinking capacity about self and life in general. In June 2021, I hired a personal fitness trainer. My team of trainers trains me two days out of the week; however, outside of those two days, one of my trainers (Holly) requires me to have two additional "purposeful movement" days to keep charged. She stated that normal active days are not purposeful but only your regular day-to-day activity. There is little to no benefit from being regularly active. Instead, having a workout routine is being intentional. She stressed the importance that having too many rest days between intentional days can be detrimental to consistency. After the third day is usually when she sees a pattern of complacency. When one becomes complacent, the progress is halted, making it hard to pick back up again. This can lead to having to start all over to recharge yourself, which is too much time wasted by then. Therefore, she stressed never taking more than two days off a regiment but always having two "purposeful movement" days to keep charged. The mind needs to be trained to keep going no matter what and enjoy the benefits of feeling good in mind and body. Exercising and eating healthy takes discipline to improve quality of life. Going to work every day requires discipline to receive full compensation. Paying bills on time is a good form of discipline to have good credit. Preparing for an athletic competition takes discipline to win a race. These are common practicalities that we should have mastered or are working on mastering. These daily practices have immediate gratifications, making them more desirable to manage, but what about spiritual discipline? It is just as necessary as any other form of discipline.

Spiritual discipline gives us access to the kingdom of God. We must understand that we need natural and spiritual discipline to obtain the results we desire to see in our lives in both worlds. Paul said in 1 Corinthians 9:27, "But I discipline my body and bring it into subjection; lest, when I have preached to others, I myself should be a disqualified." A disciplined person applies what they teach to others. Paul kept his flesh in check daily, so he did not live a partial life, failing to apply the very word he preached to others. He told his flesh what to do to maintain control over it.

The discipline principle is necessary for our relationship with the Lord. It is necessary to train the righteous man who needs a prayer life, not just prayer time, but a prayer life. Study time in the word daily and deny natural cravings. Discipline is hard and can be demanding at the same time. It can feel like it is asking too much out of us. Therefore, not too many of us like to be disciplined or even to give it.

Discipline can be harsh coming from the wrong person with the wrong intentions or depending on the offense, but God's discipline comes from a place of love. Hebrews 12:6 says, "For the Lord disciplines those He loves, and He punishes each one He accepts as His child." It is love that drives God to discipline His people. He teaches us the right way of living. This is also true for parents who teach their children the right way of living. We need discipline in every aspect of life. It is a common substance we should all want to possess. Where there is no discipline, there is no quality or self-control.

It takes self-control to become totally disciplined in every area of life. A closed mind cannot receive the necessary discipline to improve in any area. When we become open to change, we become aware that there is a lack of discipline that we seek to improve.

WILDLIFE AND WILDERNESS

A wilderness is defined as *a wild and uncultivated region, as of forest or desert, a desolated place (solitary or lonely), uninhabited or inhabited only by wild animals, a tract of wasteland, or having feelings of being abandoned by friends or by hope, deprived or destitute of inhabitants, dreary, dismal, or gloomy.* Another definition says *it is a tract of land officially designated as such and protected by the U.S. government. A wilderness is also defined as a part of a garden set apart for plants growing with unchecked luxuriance* (Dictionary.com, 2022).

From a human's perspective, wilderness is usually linked with danger. It is the inhabitance of wildlife, making man its prey to every living creature that dwells in it. I read an article from the *Insider* by Lulu Chang, *10 Safari Horror Stories That Will Chill You to the Bone*. Chang states in the article that "the purpose of wildlife preserves and safaris is to raise awareness for the receding natural habitat of the world's most beautiful and fascinating plants and animals" (Chang, 2018).

A natural wilderness can be compared with a life experience wilderness. Just as the safaris raise awareness of what dwells in it, God will also use a wilderness experience to bring awareness to where we are in our lives, where He wants us to be, and His will on the earth. As wildlife distance itself from anything structural or uneatable, this is also true regarding humankind. The more the world produces for us, a great distance comes between God and His creation.

THE DAYS OF ADAM AND NOAH

In the days of old, humankind once lived amongst the wild. Animal and man dwelled together. We see this in Adam's days and the days of Noah. On the sixth day in Genesis 1:24-31, God created man and every other living thing. God gave all dominion to man to tend to the living, i.e., plants, water beasts, bugs, birds, cattle, and field beasts. In chapter two, God called every beast of the field and air to Adam that he would name them and whatever Adam named them, that is what they would be called. He placed delightful plants in the Garden of Eden that would be pleasant for food. All creation lived amongst one another with the intent to become fruitful and populate the earth.

In the days of Noah, evil had increased so rapidly that the remembrance of God's love had decreased down to one, Noah. He was the last man standing, the only one to be found faithful in the sight of God. God had created a people with the perfection of His words, and He went unappreciated by His own creation. As evil filled the earth, God began to create His impact plan, destroy them all except Noah and his family and two of each kind of animal. In Genesis 7, God acknowledged Noah as righteous in his generation, and because Noah was obedient to God, He was able to trust Noah with the details of His impact plan to cleanse the earth from all its evil. He instructed Noah to gather two of each clean and unclean animal, one male and one female. Noah's wife, two sons, and their wives were also a part of his plan. Yes, his family reaped the benefits of his obedience to God. Noah and his family spent 40 days and nights on an ark during a storm, and after 150 days, all the water eventually receded to its bounds. He spent almost ten months with the wild in a confined space. One can only imagine the thought of being attacked by one of the unclean beasts or even the smell alone would drive me crazy. They tended to these beasts, feeding them on schedule, bathing them, and caring for them when they became ill. Noah and his family were the world's first veterinarians.

The ark can be parallel to the wilderness. The ark was designated and protected by God. Noah, his family, and the animals were set apart from the rest of the world to refine His creation. God was cultivating what He created to be life. Chang stated in her article, "as we encroach too much on these natural predators' homes, the results can quickly turn tragic" (Chang, 2018).

As we can see, the wilderness is not the most popular place anyone would desire to be in at any time, but any wilderness or wilderness experience is necessary for humankind and the beast. We need our wilderness experience to be refined and fine-tuned by God for a greater work. When God cultivates us, He brings us out of a place of compromise to uncompromised.

THE AWAKENING TO TRANSITIONING

There is a great awakening in this time. The days we live in are evil, just as they were in the days of Noah. So much so, God must call the faithful believer into isolation (a wilderness). In a spiritual sense, a wilderness is an isolated place that sets us apart from others. Though we continue to maintain interaction with others as we go on in our day to day, the heart is set apart to see things very differently; it uses discretion daily. Now it sees what God sees. The soul is illuminated, lucid with God's plan and purpose. It is like walking into a dark room, unable to see the condition of your surroundings, leaving you vulnerable to where you are. This is the unknown, and the unknown can be scary. It is not until you turn the light on where you are that your understanding is enlightened to respond to where you are standing. The room is either in disarray where you can now start cleaning and throwing away what is not beneficial, or the room is full of opulence that it takes your breath away at its sight, which you can now bask in that place and build upon it. With the lights on, you see every detail of that room. This is also with us. God will turn the lights on in your life from a wilderness experience. He will show you what has had your heart and who you have been serving as a god. It is important that we do not turn the lights off in areas where the Lord has turned the lights on. He only turns the lights on so that you may be able to respond to what you see. Discover Him in it or find Him not in it and respond accordingly. We must respond accordingly to every life experience wilderness. We must be obedient to such a place, as it is only to prepare us for what is to come. God wants to ready us for the next as He did Adam and Noah. A wilderness experience can be desolate, lonely, annoying, and frustrating. If we are not careful, we will either shorten the time there and not get the necessary pruning, or we can stay there too long and become even more blind than before going into the wilderness.

TIMING IN THE WILDERNESS

God set a time for every wilderness experience, though we cannot figure out the set time on our own nor how much time the assignment requires. However, we can consider ones like John the Baptist. There is no question that he was unique in his own right. John the Baptist wore odd clothing, ate strange food, and preached an unusual message to the Judeans who came to see him. He was the announcer of the coming Messiah. He had one preaching theme, and that was repentance. He confronted fearlessly, and he lived an uncompromising life. Now, John the Baptist was a voice in the wilderness. With the magnitude of his assignment, he lived in the wilderness. He did not have seasons of it, but it was life. It is how he functioned daily. He stood for the truth all the time. So, we learn through his life that when standing for the truth, friends and family will abandon you. People around you will think twice before befriending you. Your inner circle becomes far and few. In fact, the Bible only speaks of one good friend of John the Baptist, and that was Jesus. Not having an inner circle of friends is also considered a wilderness experience. Others in the Bible had wilderness experiences that were only seasonal. Noah was there for ten months. Israel's was intended for seven days, but their murmuring and disbelief in God hindered their stay, and they lingered much longer than planned. Jesus' wilderness experience was for forty days.

Focus is pivotal while in the wilderness. This is for God to accomplish His work fully and aligning with God, becoming single-minded to understand what He is doing. If we do otherwise, it could cause great distress in our lives.

As I journeyed in my wilderness, observing what was happening, I realized I was just transitioning. A wilderness is transitioning out of one place to another. Jesus' wilderness prepared Him to make the greatest transition of all times. Even He expressed deep agony and sorrow in His Wilderness. He alone shows us that it is not an easy place to be in. If you aren't listening properly, what you hear could bring great distress. Fear will try to settle in, and on a serious note, you will try to reason with God, as Jesus did. In my wilderness, God was undoing, removing, and replacing.

REMOVING AND REPLACING

The concept of removing and replacing is evident when making a conscience decision to introduce change. Years ago, my routine doctor's visit came with unwelcome news. After having blood work weeks before the appointment, the results were in. All my levels and rates were good except for my low cholesterol (the bad cholesterol). It was slightly over the normal count. My doctor's immediate solution was medication without even educating me on what was causing it to be abnormal. I did what any self-advocator would do. I declined the medication and asked her what causes bad cholesterol. Now, in my family, it is generic to have bad cholesterol, but no one had the knowledge of what was causing it. The unhealthy habits that I developed from childhood obviously were still present in my life. The doctor named fatty foods that cause bad cholesterol, which I had to find my poison. She stated, "Fast foods, junk food, fried foods." All these habits I had already eliminated. I was thinking, what could it be. Lastly, she said cold cuts (processed meats). My awareness lights flashed immediately, and I said, "That's it!" At this time, I worked in Corporate America from nine to five, getting two little girls off to school, and processed meats, i.e., hotdogs, bologna, and salami, seemed much easier when trying to carry the world on your shoulders. Eating something fast, easy, and on the go was more of an option for me than taking the time to cook something more balanced. Also, during this time, I was not a huge fan of fruits and vegetables. I did not know how to enjoy them whenever I did try them. Once I identified my poison, I went home with a new mindset. I had to figure out how I wanted to continue my nutritional journey. I had an epitome that when I removed the fatty foods, I did not replace them with power foods. If I wanted my cholesterol to be normal and to stay normal, I could not just eliminate the bad foods, but I had to add foods that would benefit my body as I got older. During this time, I began eating more salads and making fruit bowls, and most importantly, I learned how to enjoy power foods. When change presents itself, be prepared to examine where you are in the moment, identify the flaws, and be okay with fixing them by putting a new plan in place.

Four years ago, Naomi Dowdy wrote an article in Charisma Magazine called *4 Keys to How God Brings Transition*. In Deuteronomy 7:22, God told the Israelites through Moses, "You will not be allowed to eliminate them all at once, or the wild animals will multiply around you." The New King James Version says, "Lest the beast of the field become too numerous for you." God would drive their enemies out slowly so they would not become more vulnerable to the animals. It is clear the Israelites are no longer living in the days of Noah, where man could dwell with the beast. The evil in the world plays a big part in this change.

Dowdy says, "Instead of speedily eliminating the opposition, God wants to remove and replace. He will do this with attitudes, mind-sets, circumstances, relationships, and anything else that would keep you from being fully prepared and equipped to possess the promises He has given you. For example, where you are afraid, He will orchestrate a situation that will help you overcome your fear and replace it with faith" (Dowdy, 2013). I realized this is what was taking place in my life. God was removing old ideologies taught to me while growing up and learned today. God was making me more equipped for what lay ahead. Everything that was there as a hindrance had to be recognized and replaced with things that would help me on the journey. God wants to make us wise and strong in Him. He wants to train us to have an ear to hear and not be fearful of our enemies. The life-changing experience of a wilderness season will bring evident change, and one must always remain thankful and learn patience in the process of change.

Chapter One

WHEN GOD INTERRUPTS YOUR NORMAL

The average Christian today has a weekly routine that we vigorously follow. We work a job, go to school, care for children, serve on church committees, attend or lead prayer once a week, and, of course, church every Sunday for most religions. Nothing can come between these routines. It is all we know to be normal for believers, and it will always be what we do. We fail to realize that through these routines, the ones that ought to bring glory to God do not. Instead, these routines may just also serve as a sense of belonging, becoming props to boost our self-esteem. Now, it is okay to commit to obligations or contribute to be a part of the solution, but we should never leave the ideal of putting God first in all we do. There should still be an awakening to the Spirit of Christ that will allow Him to shift us around seasons. We develop horrible feelings when missing one of these weekly routines, and they are unimaginable. You feel like you are not dedicated as you should be, you broke a big promise, you cannot be relied on, and others who rely on you may second guess your level of commitment. These crazy thoughts will run through your head until you fulfill your next weekly commitment. Now things are back to normal. However, we are sadly mistaken if we think this is God's only ideal of committing to Him. Commitment means involving yourself, engaging, pledging, or promising. When we committed our lives to Christ, we committed to engaging with Him regularly, to involve ourselves in any of His affairs. We pledged to fulfill the greater work and promised to serve Him all the days of our lives. This commitment is not limited to the four walls of the church.

What do you do when God interrupts your normal routine? He alters your entire life, changes appointments, cancels trips, stops engagements, and even removes friends. What you thought was a normal routine, the time is up for it. He is doing things differently. What do you do? Do you resist the season of change and continue as you know? This is easy for us to do because not only are routines props, but that also means they make you feel safe and secure. Or do you submit to what God is doing and let it all go and let the change happen? Do not fight against it; just go with it. This is the hard path for most believers. Why? "I'm doing these things unto the Lord!" If that is the case, it should be easy to shift when He says to "shift" or go higher when He says, "go higher." It is hard because we do not believe God will change our routine. After all, the reality is that we have put all hope in them.

Let us take the first disciples as an example of a normal routine being interrupted, and let us examine their response. The gospel, according to Mark 1:16-20, says Jesus was walking along the shore of Galilee. While he walked, He spotted Simon, who is called Peter, and his brother Andrew. They were in a boat fishing. Fishing during this time was prominent, and it was common to fish with a net. It was one of the biggest industries around the Sea of Galilee. This may have been Peter and his brother Andrew's normal as they fished for a living. I'm quite sure this was one of their many everyday routines. But in verse seventeen, something was about to change their routine quickly. "Jesus called out to them, 'Come, follow me, and I will show you how to fish for people!'" Verse eighteen shows their remarkable response to Jesus, "And they left their nets at once and followed Him." How easy was it for them to just follow Him, not having proof of who He was and the details of this strategy to fish for people? They made it look relatively easy. Without question, they followed. They were bored with their routine and wanted a new normal. We reach such a point in our lives where we are waiting for change. This is a good place to be when serving the Lord. Always stay ready for the next and the new.

In Mark 1, he further explains the next disciple. Jesus continues up the shore with His two new disciples, and He now sees two more brothers. James and John, Zebedee's sons. In verse twenty, Jesus gives them the same petition, "He called them at once, and they also followed Him, leaving their father in the boat." An even more remarkable response. James and John's tenaciousness can teach us the valuable lesson of the risk of leaving family when following Christ. We try to take them with us, but Jesus called James and John, and not their father. It shows a great deal of seriousness when you sacrifice leaving your loved ones. It is no different from enlisting in the army, there is a price, and you must count the cost before making such a huge commitment.

When I re-dedicated my life to the Lord in 2001, my life changed at the snap of a finger. I no longer fit in a place that was normal to me, and eventually, I left my family. The lines of communication completely stopped. Before turning my life around, my mother and I would go to breakfast every Saturday, and I would entertain idle conversations. I had reached a point in my life that I could not take it anymore and my normal changed. I felt bad at one point and could not understand why. It was guilt for not wanting to be around the negativity. It was not until I read this chapter in Mark about James and John leaving their father in the boat to follow Christ that my decision to separate from my family was validated. I received my peace, and I was able to continue pressing forward in Christ.

Another fitting example of God interrupting a normal routine is 1 Kings 19:19. Elijah was given a special strength from the Lord in 1 Kings

18:46, to run on foot to Jezreel to beat the rain as he delivered a message. On the way, he found Elisha tending to his routine. Elisha was a very wealthy farmer. Elijah found him plowing in the field with his team. Elijah makes a swift move by going to Elisha and placing a cloak on his shoulder. A cloak or mantle served a vast of purposes at that time, and it was an essential piece of clothing. Elijah placing the cloak on Elisha's shoulders was symbolic that he would be his successor. Elisha's response was slightly different from the disciples. In verse twenty, Elisha says, "First let me go kiss my father and mother good-bye, and then I will go with you." Elisha did not go right away like the disciples; he had to spend a little more time with his family and team. Elijah was quite patient with him as he advised him to go back but think about what he had just done to him. In other words, count the cost. Elijah had to kill an ox, and by doing this, he made a strong commitment to follow Elijah. He would never be able to return to his wealthy farmer's lifestyle.

We would not even think of making a sacrifice that would cause us to leave our wealth to follow someone else. This is not an easy thing to do. All the disciples answered Jesus in the same way. Elisha's response was a little different, like responses today. We may question or falter, but we should never stop following Christ.

DREAMS & VISIONS

Dreams and visions can be associated with God's way of communicating with His people. This is no surprise as there are individuals in the Old and New Testament whom God foretold or gave foresight. Dreams usually occur when one is sleeping, and visions occur when one is awake, they both can be involuntary.

To understand dreams and visions more, I purchased a book by Jim W. Goll called *The Seer, The Prophetic Power of Visions, Dream, and Open Heavens*. Goll provides insight into dream language and its importance.

Our dreams are only one way of God speaking to believers. He also speaks through visions and trances. Joseph had a dream in Genesis 37, Daniel had a vision in Daniel 7, and Paul was taken into a trance in Acts 22:17-18. He reveals Himself through one of these avenues. "If there is a prophet among you, I, the Lord, shall make Myself known to him in a vision. I shall speak with him in a dream" (Numbers 13:6).

Here are examples of biblical dreams:

- Daniel is an Old Testament prophet who received dreams from the Lord.
- In Genesis 15:12-17, God speaks to Abraham in a dream regarding the centuries of slavery his descendants would face in Egypt and their deliverance to the Promised Land.
- In Genesis 28:10-19, Jacob saw a ladder extending into heaven with angels ascending and descending.
- In Daniel 2:1-49, Nebuchadnezzar was one of the evilest rulers during his time; nonetheless, he received a dream from God that he so desperately wanted its meaning.
- In Matthew 27:19, Pilate's wife, during Jesus' trial, received a warning through a dream that Jesus was indeed a righteous man.
- In Genesis 37:5-11, Joseph had a dream symbolizing that he would rule over his brothers and parents and that they would bow to him.

There are more examples in the Bible. Dreams and visions are biblical and of God.

I started having odd dreams at the tender age of five. I learned to interpret them then by simply describing what I saw when I was young. I did my best to explain the details to my older sister. The only thing is, I did not know God was talking to me. I had no way of knowing how to connect them to God. It was not until I became older and saved that I realized this was God. I started to pay more attention to what I saw by recording them on paper.

In the early 2000's I had my first vision. I was walking to work in downtown Milwaukee, and as I was walking through the skywalk, a snapshot of a young Black lady appeared before me. She had a big puffy ponytail on top of her head. I saw her for about thirty seconds and then she went away. I had no idea what was happening. So, I went on with my day.

God will use visions to show His concern for us. One of the important lessons in seeing visions of other people is that you are required to do something. It was not until later that week that I realized God was speaking to me concerning this young lady. I became even more in tune with them after that.

JUMP TO SAVE YOUR LIFE

Every dream recording in the Bible was God's way of informing His people of what was next or a warning as a preventive measure to avoid impending danger. One thing is for sure, whatever God shows a dreamer, it should change their life drastically. Dreams and visionaries must act on what the Lord reveals to them. Failure to yield to God's supernatural way of communicating could result in forfeiting new opportunities.

On December 5, 2016, I received a life-altering dream. This would be the dream that transitioned me into my wilderness experience. The dream was so startling that I did not record it until December 18, 2016. During this time, I served at a local church where I had been worshipping for sixteen years. This was the church that God used to set me free from the bondage of my flesh. There I learned relationship and worship. For the last few years, I had served the leaders as an armor bearer and an assistant pastor. The ministry was going through so many changes; members began falling away; however, the leaders remained committed to their duties as pastors.

On December 5, 2016, my life was interrupted by God's supernatural instructions. My weekly routine was set, and I found comfort in it.

However, in the dream, I saw the end of a road at the peak of the sky. Behind me was a gray open portal. I could not see people, but I sensed familiar people around me. My daughters were on my left and right (they were much younger). There was a force there helping us put on jackets. The force showed me what lever to pull before we got closer to earth. It was then that I realized we had to jump. I remember hearing the words parachute and life support was the purpose of the jackets. Before I knew it, we jumped. We were falling from the pinnacle of the sky. I remember questioning where we would land, and the force was with us as we were falling. It reminded me of the jackets. Once I sat down to ponder the dream, the Lord spoke so clearly.

The dream as interpreted on Dec 18th...

> *Holy Spirit was the force there with me. He is preparing me for a transition.*
>
> *He is showing me that I have reached the end of something and must jump from this world to a new place. It is time for me to jump into my new season and leave a place behind. I believe that when I make this jump, doors will open for me. I believe my eldest daughter, who ran away from me at 16 years old, will return to me.*
>
> *I will try and talk my way out of this to avoid having to take such a frightful journey.*
>
> *I will doubt and question God along the way, but He is going to remind me of the tools He provided for the change.*
>
> *I will be afraid along the way and even when I get there. I will not trust the new place, the people, or anything else that will come with it, but I must trust God. He has assured me that He will take care of me.*

As I was writing this section (March 25, 2020), I realized that part of the dream interpretation had come to pass. My daughter, who ran away from home at sixteen, returned to me on February 11, 2020 (prophecy fulfilled). She is now 25 years old; a mother/daughter book collaboration is expected to come out of that season of our lives.

February 28, 2017, I removed myself from the church where I had been fellowshipping for sixteen years and where I collaborated closely with the leaders during Sunday worship and Tuesday night Walking in the Word Services.

Every spiritual encounter with God requires action. It is never to see the vision and do nothing with it but to ponder it in our hearts, ask God for clarity, and simply move with Him. This takes faith, discipline, and trust in God. For every transition, there is a due season. Galatians 6:9 says, "And let us not grow weary while doing good, for in due season we shall reap if we do not lose heart." This is a strong message. Transitioning is not a comfortable ride because you have extraordinarily little insight into the journey. It requires your energy, time, talent, and your undivided attention. It is challenging work. Remaining faithful can be a challenge when we are not fully aware of the plan. To be weary means to become mentally or physically exhausted. It means impatient or dissatisfied with something.

Moses worked extremely hard in the wilderness under God's counsel. In Exodus, he pronounced the ten plagues over Egypt, instituted the Passover, consecrated all the firstborns of Israel, and led Israel into the wilderness, crossing them over a Sea. He defeated the Amalekites and established Israel's civil, moral, and spiritual laws, making the Tabernacle and the priestly garments. He had his hands full the moment he was called until he died. Moses became exhausted by Israel's fickleness. He was dissatisfied with their murmuring and complaining. In Numbers 20:7-10, Moses became angry at Israel. They were tired and thirsty from the journey and wanted water. The Lord gave Moses and Aaron the instructions to get the rod (authority) and speak to a rock, and the rock would provide water. However, Moses did not heed God's counsel. He was already weary, and he gave a weary response. Instead of speaking to the rock, he struck the rock with the rod out of anger and took credit for providing water (miracle).

It displeased God. In verse twelve, God told Moses he would only see the promise but would not enter it. This did not disqualify him as a prophet. God continued to use Moses and loved on him. Moses only missed his due season by not being able to enter the Promised Land, though he accomplished tasks in his time.

The importance of Moses' life is that we can miss our due seasons if we do not carefully follow the plan of God. He is holy, and we must treat Him as such. "And let us not grow weary while doing good, for, in due season, we shall reap if we do not lose heart." Moses did good in his time. He made a vast number of mistakes, as we all do. Though life was challenging for him, the work set before him was great. He was doing good because God was faithful to His promises to him.

The wilderness can be challenging, and it can bring heartache, which does not mean you are not doing good. If we know God is with us, we should always uphold the thought that we are doing well. This posture gives us the motivation and strength to continue for the reaping in due season.

As we only see part of the matter. Paul said it best in 1 Corinthians 13:9, "For we know in part, and we prophesy in part." If God knows the whole plan, that alone is enough to trust His plan for our lives.

QUARANTINED BY GOD

"Come, my people, enter your chambers, and shut your doors behind you; Hide yourself, as it were, for a little moment, until the indignation is past. For behold, the Lord comes out of His place to punish the inhabitants of the earth for their iniquity; the earth will also disclose her blood and will no longer cover her slain" (Isaiah 26:20-21). In this passage, God was urging His people to take refuge from the coming judgment. Isaiah was the prophet He used to call the nation of Judah back to Himself and tell of salvation through the coming Messiah. His people had sinned against Him greatly, and Isaiah was the voice of reasoning in his time. Today's world is much like it was then; as evil grows by the second, it displeases the Lord as it did in the days of old. It seems in Isaiah 26:20-21 that the Lord was calling the nations into quarantine, isolation, or a wilderness season, to bring judgment against the evil on the earth. An event like this also took place during the time of the Passover in Exodus 12 before the death of the firstborns of Egypt. The Lord spoke to Moses and instructed him to take lambs according to the size of his family, kill them and mix the blood with bitter hyssop and use the blood to mark his doorpost. Now Moses was an advisor for the people, so these instructions were for all of Israel. The blood was a sign that when the death angel passed through the land, he would pass over the house. The blood was a protection from the plague that the Lord had released on the earth (Psalm 91:1,4).

God had begun the process of delivering Israel out of Egypt. He was incredibly detailed about how He wanted His people postured while He was at work in the land (Exodus 12:1-11). The timing of this book amazes me. My wilderness season was from 2017 to 2019; however, I am writing during such a historical time in the current world. The Lord has released a plague in the land today that is claiming the lives of so many, COVID-19 (Corona Virus). My heart goes out to all who have lost a loved one, friend, neighbor, co-worker, or companion.

This disease was first discovered in December 2019 in Wuhan, China, and by January 2020, it had reached the United States of America and 197 other countries by March 2020. The disease has caused a collective interruption, interfering with major events worldwide, graduations, schools, sporting games, proms, birthdays, and church sessions. Whatever our normal was, it has been completely placed on hold until further notice. Students were ready to graduate or finish the semester to advance to the next grade. I personally was getting ready for a trip to Kenya, Africa, and my youngest daughter's prom. These two events were so important. I was excited and anticipating both events. However, God's plans were different from mine. Everything was canceled. I looked at the bright side of all of this. It sure saved me money! But the world now is in limbo, isolation, quarantined, or wilderness. This catastrophic disease has forced the nations into isolation to control the spread of this virus, and we collectively had to practice social distancing. The new wilderness is now called Social Distancing. There were so many speculations that COVID-19 was transmitted by touch for a period or airborne for a length of time. It was discovered to be more vulnerable to the older generations and/or individuals with pre-existing health conditions. COVID-19 exposed bad eating practices and lack of exercise within the African American community. Though we do not know God's purpose for this disease, we know that He uses this disease to bring discipline to all creation. Like the plague in Egypt, it targeted the firstborns of Egypt as it was a part of the Lord's plan to free His people from bondage.

Today, God has socially distanced His people and called us to a place of seeking Him. He is bringing us to our knees. When God interrupts our plans, He is trying to get our attention. He is trying to do something bigger than a trip to Africa, prom, graduation, the political race, and any other major event. He removes all distractions from us and alters our normal. The question is, are we listening? Or have we established new idols or continued with the idols in our homes, i.e., social media, electronic devices, food, or poor thinking. God wants to do a new thing.

ELIMINATING THE MIDDLEMAN

In different life journeys, we all had a go-between or mediator at a point in our lives. Jesus is and will always be our mediator. He is the one who stands between the Father and us that we may be reconciled back to Him from our sins and escape the Father's wrath. A middleman is an agent or an intermediary or a go-between. We rely on this person as a tutor in new seasons to help us grow to the next level. This person possesses a level of wise counsel, might, and pure intentions. We submit to them, trusting that they hear from the Lord or have an elevated level of experience. We glean from these people; we challenge them with questions and learn to do what we do not understand. They are necessary for their seasons, but one thing is for sure, that agent was not designed to stay with you forever. They are only equipped for a season. When their time is up, it is up, and there is nothing you can do about it but adapt and adjust quickly to walking on your own.

The Laws of Moses are parallel to an agent. The children of Israel entered their new season after they escaped from Egypt. They had to learn to adapt to the new in that new place. They could no longer rely on the provision in bondage or the direction from a wicked leader, but now they must learn to put their hope and trust in God through His leaders. The biggest mistake we all make on both sides of the agent and the student is trying to hang on to them for a lifetime when God has only called them to get you to a certain point in your life. If your agent is not challenging you to trust more and stand on your own, you are in danger of destruction and completely losing that relationship. Intermediaries will become co-dependent on the student because they are depended upon for knowledge which brings that leader fulfillment. A go-between could be your pastor, mentor, teacher, counselor, or friend. We must always keep in mind that all these roles are held by humans. They are human, too, and susceptive to falling or getting it wrong. Your total reliance should not be on that person. We admire them for the sacrifices and work they do but never put them in the place where God belongs. "Don't put your confidence in powerful people: there is no help for you there" (Psalm 146:3). Help from man is temporal and inconsistent, but help from God is lasting and effective.

When God interrupted Elisha's normal while he worked at his family's farm, he was met by his agent, Elijah. Elijah would become his agent to show Elisha the wonders of God, but most importantly, he had to teach Elisha how to be committed to the work of God. Elisha came from a well-rounded and established family; therefore, he already possessed a great willingness to serve in any capacity. He, however, had to learn God's way. When the Lord took Elijah up to heaven (2 Kings 2:11) by the whirlwind, He separated the two. Elijah's seasons were up on the earth, and as Elisha's agent. This is symbolic of removing the agent. Elisha, too, was a prophet who knew his master's time had ended. Therefore, he stood ready to continue all he had learned from his master. He even built upon Elijah's achievements. This is how we should all stand when the Lord begins to remove those significant roles from around us. We should not attempt to hold on to them and continue in their shadows but embrace the change and posture ourselves to continue what we have learned through those significant lives.

Jesus and His disciples are another notable example of when God removes your middleman. Jesus handpicked his disciples in an abbreviated time. He was the master teacher to the first twelve, knowing that He would leave them to the work He started one day, just as Elijah knew when his time was ending that God handpicked Elisha (2 Kings 19:16) to be his successor. Neither one of them tried to save their relationship. There were much more weightier matters Elisha would have to tend to by the leading of God.

Jesus and His disciples went about different cities performing miracles and wonders of God. They asked Him questions and followed all His demands. They grew fond of Him, developing a strong brotherly love, and when He ascended to heaven, the disciples did not know what to do with themselves. They went back to what they were found doing when Jesus called them; they went fishing (John 21:3), and Peter led them. Metaphorically, Jesus was the middleman, the agent who would teach the twelve how to commit their lives to God's work. The disciples would eventually learn that they were now the frontline workers. They had to learn to engage in the same work they saw the Master engage in, maintaining the same character, commitment, discipline, will, and desire He had to perform His Father's will. Elijah was a tutor, and the law was a tutor (Galatians 3:24). Jesus functioned as a tutor; however, the middleman is to bring us to Christ so that we might be justified by faith (Galatians 3:24).

This is not to dismiss any leadership roles in the church, as the Lord gives gifts to each of us to equip the body of Christ for the divine work, edifying the church that the work would not falter (Ephesians 4:11-13). Therefore, we must be led by God when serving under others as intentions are not pure but selfish, which could stunt your growth in God.

Are you only growing in church work? If so, church work is not necessarily growing in God. However, it does prove you have grown in character, but there is much more to be discovered. As we grow in the Lord, we experience an unexplainable growth spurt: "a tremendous amount of growth in a brief period of time or a rapid rise in height and weight" (Dictionary.com, 2022). We are like sunlight and water on the fertilized ground when we are plugged into God as our source. It is okay to esteem and admire one another, but never idolize them to the point that they are all you see. God will place leaders in your life for a season and remove them. Relying on that relationship more than relying on God will make it hard for you when God removes them. The desperation of staying in the relationship will cause one to become an obstacle that will affect your growth in the Lord. It will slow down your ability to grow personally and privately with God. Constantly having a person above us hinders our ability to grow.

If you are not growing in God, in the Word, in revelation, or faith, there is a possibility you are disconnected from the power source (Jesus) and connected to the wrong middleman. You may want to examine where you are currently planted in life, check your surroundings, who you are submitted to, and examine their intentions.

Leaders must be more conscious of this pattern and be careful not to become a stumbling block to the flock subconsciously or unconsciously. Leaders sometimes lack within themselves, and they use their flock as a prop, keeping their flock beneath them so that they feel above them to block their growth. Leaders must be careful not to stand in the way of someone else's ability to grow. Be careful not to block someone's growth spurt (rapid growth) with God.

Prayer: Heavenly Father, as You raise us into a place of leadership, help us, dear Lord, not to stand in the way of anyone developing and going beyond parameters and borders with You. I pray leaders will not stand in the way of Your people experiencing rapid growth, from experiencing a rapid rise in height and weight supernatural, and from experiencing tremendous growth in a brief period. You are their God. Thank You that You gave them their mind to study the scripture for themselves and to gain wisdom for themselves through You. Help us not to stand in Your way.

Titles and positions will also cause us to lose focus. When I think about Nebuchadnezzar, he knew there were abilities he did not possess, so he relied on Daniel. Jesus had a plethora of abilities, and in all His abilities, He demonstrated ministry, apostle, prophet, evangelist, pastor, and teacher. He demonstrated all the offices of God, and then He transferred the power to the disciples and said, "Now you go out as I did." He did not stunt their growth. He did not stand in the way. He was a teacher; He taught them everything He knew. He made a spirit transaction and handed down abilities, powers, and anointing.

The work should never be hoarded. There is so much work to be done, there is much to go around, but the laborers are few. Therefore, we do not have to trample over or compete over who is doing what and how. We also should not covet what someone else is doing or has. God will give us our appointed assignment and transfer power to do it. God will transfer the power to do it despite our shortcomings and insecurities and thinking that we cannot do it. Jesus transferred power and authority to the disciples by training them and teaching them. There was a season when they had to learn, listen, humble themselves and be quiet. They had to study Christ's life to show themselves approved, that when the time came for them to go out, Jesus got out of their way at the appointed time. He did not try to keep the position of power to Himself on the earth. He told them in Luke 22 that it would be far better when He left because greater works they would go on to do. Jesus set an expectation, and He set the bar HIGH.

There was a time in my life when I struggled with this expectation because I did not understand how anyone could do greater than the Messiah.

I was so insecure that I could not see what Jesus was saying here. I was bothered until Holy Spirit gave me wisdom, and I then knew that His power would no longer be limited to one household or region, but many will be filled with the power of the Holy Spirit (Yah breath) throughout all the earth at once. Jesus was not afraid to end His season in the flesh, but it was only the beginning. He now works through His vessels. His fruit and labor are still running on the earth and will for generations to come.

If you are serving under leaders who are not challenging you to grow, are not challenging your wrong decisions, and do not allow you to become hands-on with the work, I encourage you to pray and ask God to show you your exodus.

> *Prayer: Lord, keep our hearts humble and our ears open to hear You. Bless those who are ready to speak that all may hear the truth. Thank You for the growth spurt, the rapid rise in height and weight in Your glory, and a tremendous amount of growth in a brief period in the spirit. It will not be church as usual!*

Chapter Two

THE WILDERNESS' PURPOSE

In Exodus 5:1, Moses' and Aaron's first encounter with Pharaoh regarding the release of Israel says, "Let My people go, that they may hold a feast to Me in the wilderness." In verse three, the Hebrews pleaded with Pharaoh saying, "Please, let us go three days' journey into the desert and sacrifice to the Lord our God." I studied Exodus many times, but I did not fully grasp this wilderness concept. The wilderness is not a bad place to be in, but it is a place that the Spirit will lead us to prepare us for days, weeks, months, or life's journey. God established the wilderness as a place for communion with His people, the ones He adores and calls His own. The wilderness is a place to offer sacrifices to the Lord, to give thanks, and even praise Him daily for His goodness and provision. The agenda in the wilderness is not us, but God is the agenda. Israel missed it, and so did I during my wilderness season. God told Moses to tell Pharaoh to let His people go so they could have a feast for Him in the wilderness. The Hebrew leaders pleaded, oh, please can we go to the desert (a dry place) to offer sacrifices to the Lord. Once again, God was the agenda. He was the total focus of the wilderness because no one on their own would want to go to a dry place for any reason.

The wilderness will be a dry place. We may grow weary, faint, deprived of the outside world, or feel alone and abandoned. These all represent dryness. However, we must trust God for His daily provision. God is intentional in everything He does, and He was quite intentional when He made the wilderness a desert-like place. I think the common things in life compete with God and sometimes make it exceedingly difficult for us to trust only in Him.

Therefore, the dry place is necessary, and the stripping is necessary. Bringing us out of our comfort zone is necessary. When we are not used to the dryness and do not understand its importance, we can easily begin trying to create our own provision. That is when we become defiant in the wilderness and crafty at making idols in the mind or externally.

We should always be prepared to experience deficiency or an absence of something in the wilderness. We must be careful not to try and find something else to fulfill those dry areas. One thing is for sure, the wilderness is very trying. If we are not careful to walk with the Lord while in such a place and do as He requested of us, we could miss the Spirit's flow, and when the Spirit flows, the blessings of the Lord flow.

Offering sacrifices to Him in today's time is fasting and praying. Otherwise, we could end up like Israel in their wilderness for 40 years after four hundred years in Egypt (bondage), denying ourselves of anything that brings us delight.

The COVID-19 period brought a great depression to the world. Fear and panic settled in the hearts, causing the masses to put their hope and trust on daily essential items. At the beginning of this pandemic, people were crowding the stores and overstocking supplies. You could see the selfish nature of humanity. It is amazing how an epidemic can expose man's true nature and heart. The people's hearts grew loveless, not caring if there were enough supplies on the shelf for everyone considering we were all going through the same pandemic. Matthew 24 speaks of times like this; however, it is not yet declaring the end. Verse twelve says, "Sin will be rampant everywhere, and the love of many will grow cold." This pandemic revealed the loveless nature of man and where their hearts were truly set. We should be more conscious of others during times like this, joining together and showing concern for one another.

A CALL TO WORSHIP

I mentioned before that a wilderness place is not a bad place to be in. The wilderness can bring a great deal of favor if we go through it properly. Having the favor of God gives us the permission to ask anything, assured that we will receive. However, if we choose to rest on our own understanding, we become so afflicted with anxieties and the pressures of life that we lose focus on what God is doing in the present moment. I saw my wilderness season as an invitation. God invited me to enter a dry season, a place from all the normal necessities to a place of communion with Him. This is a private call. Though it affects us collectively, the Lord deals with us individually.

In Exodus 7:16, God gave another message to Moses and Aaron to deliver to Pharaoh concerning the release of Israel. He told them to tell Pharaoh, "The Lord, the God of the Hebrews, has sent me to tell you, 'Let my people go so that they can worship me in the wilderness.'" Worships means having a deep respect and paying homage to God. God was using Israel's wilderness to please Himself. He wanted Israel to pay homage to Him as He was their God. And we have the same nature as God. We please ourselves when we dress our children up and make them look nice. We teach them certain guidelines, and when they follow them, we are fulfilled. This was God's position with Israel. Though their wilderness journey had plenty of purposes, God wanted His children to bring glory and honor to His name, but that was hard for Israel, so it still is today for us.

Our wilderness seasons are God calling us to worship Him in spirit and truth (John 4:24). God is a spirit, and we must worship Him as such. Not with money, works, or rituals, but this is when God wants our minds and hearts. He wants our commitment to Him. When God requires us to commit our hearts to Him, He again wants to please Himself. To worship Him is to honor Him with our lives.

Exodus 28 was the making of the priestly garments. After Israel's release from bondage, God began to establish His expectation for Israel. He had to teach them how to live under His statutes and ordinances. This was necessary, considering they were under Pharaoh's counsel for forty years. In chapter 28, God had to teach Israel how to worship Him. Verse one says, "Now take Aaron your brother, and his sons with him, from among the children of Israel, that he may minister to Me as priest, Aaron, and Aaron's sons…" The Levites were the priests God would use to oversee the Tabernacle's operations and assist Israel with maintaining a relationship with God. Look how, in this verse, God reveals that they would minister to Him as priests. This passage was so enlightening when I studied Exodus during my wilderness period in 2017.

Through this passage, I realized that when we operate in the gifts and abilities God has given us, we are ministering to Him. We are waiting on Him. As we serve the people, we are first serving Him. We cater to His plans for every assignment. Ministering means to do for, help, answer or attend. What are you doing for God in your life? Are you helping the gospel to reach the unreachable? Have you answered the call to take up your cross and follow Him, and are you applying yourself or present with God every waking day of your life? Not just on Sunday, but every day.

TIME TO LISTEN AND INQUIRE

The wilderness also requires the believer to listen. This is when we should have an overabundance of quiet time with the Lord. We need the wisdom of God to know what He expects from us in the moment and to know wisdom for the future. Surely, God has not called us to such times of uncertainties and not have a plan. Therefore, we must have a heart to listen to God, not people and the news, to keep up with what is going on in the world. We should not even listen to our disbelief but pay close keen attention to what the Lord says. He then will lead you to the answer through an earthly resource. Through this knowledge, we gain the confidence to continue with His plans. No matter if people may oppose it or try not to make sense of it, we gain confidence in the voice of God when we take the time to listen to Him directly. That is what Jesus did, and when He transcended, the disciples had to practice the same independence on the voice of God. Paul provided warnings of false prophets and false teaching in his letters, as Jesus also warned us to beware of them.

COVID-19 urged leaders everywhere to press in to hear God. During this period, every church operation shut down, and church was streamed through technology. It appeared that God had forsaken the assemblies for a season. Now, why would God interfere with something that brings Him glory? Could it be God was not pleased with the direction the church has journeyed? Over time, has the church become increasingly loveless, leaning on its own understanding? Therefore, was COVID-19 to get the attention back to God's original plan for the body of Christ? For far too long, the church has pushed its agenda and pushed back God's agenda. Believers are building brands rather than building the Kingdom of God. The nations have placed God on the back burner. Race, religion, and prejudice have been the priority causing the church to become challenged like never before.

Every September, I traditionally go on a 21-day fast to seek God for the coming year. During my fast in 2017, I sat at my bedside, meditating on God for the season. While I sat there, the Lord showed me a vision of a train on a fast track. I looked down on the train while it moved at maximum speed. I could see the track it was riding on as it was a straight path, but as the train approached a particular part of the tracks, another track veered slightly to the right. I came out of the vision right when the train reached that point of the track. Immediately I began to inquire of the Lord. When we inquire of God, we choose to believe God and not lean on our own understanding. To inquire means to seek, ask, or investigate. I did not understand what I saw, so I investigated it and asked the Lord. As I waited, I heard the Spirit say, "The opposing path." From that, He gave me more understanding. He revealed to me that the nature of man is like a train. My nature was like that train. When we begin to walk with the Lord and commit a life to serve Him, our zeal and dedication put us on a fast track to rapid growth in Him. We rapidly grow in the works of God, and He is obligated to perfect the works of our hands. However, the further we go in Him, we become prideful and veer off His path. And when we veer off the path, we take on our own agenda and leave God's agenda. The second path of the track was a symbol of pride. It represented a veering, a detour, or an agenda. This happens to most believers and churches everywhere, we start zealously for God, careful to follow Him, but we lose momentum for His will along the way and eventually go our own way. Once pride settles in, there is a gain of a false sense of momentum. Like that train in the vision, if it chooses the opposing path, it will continue at maximum speed. However, it will miss what God had planned for it on the right path. The opposing path leaves the train very much vulnerable to anything and ill-equipped for the journey.

When you do not hear anything from God, do not do anything. And if you hear something, evaluate it, and ask yourself, is this godly, or is it God-inspired? If it is not God, it will not prosper. I remember in 2018, I really desired to be in a relationship, and it just did not seem like it was going to happen anytime soon. So, I decided to help God out (a bad idea) by trying a dating website. I inquired of the Lord and did not hear, but I did it anyway because of my own desires. The dating site required a credit card number for a monthly fee. I was initially reluctant, but my desperation for a relationship overrode my reservations, and I did it. I put my card in, and immediately it drafted two payments from my account. I was utterly shocked and regretful. I could not get angry because I did not yield to God's silence. God did not say anything for me to listen to. He kept completely silent; therefore, I should have done nothing. It was then I learned a big lesson that when God is silent and there are no instructions to follow, trust His silence and be still as He sees and knows all things.

We must trust our Godly instincts when in the wilderness. Like Isaiah, who heard God and whatever he heard, lived his life based on the things he heard from the heavens. We can hear clearly when our hearts and affections are set on the things above. However, we cannot hear properly if our hearts are not settled in heaven.

Chapter Three

FOR THE MAKING

Olive oil production begins with harvesting olives. After harvesting, the olives are washed to remove dirt, leaves, and twigs. Once the twigs are filtered out, they are ready for processing into oil. The first stage in the oil-making process is crushing, during which the olives are reduced to a paste by a crushing device in a gentle fashion—the process of crushing tears the flesh cells to facilitate the oil to release. The paste is then mixed for 20-45 minutes, allowing the small oil droplets to combine into bigger ones (growth and productivity). Heat and water are added to the paste to increase its yielding. Extended mixing time will also increase the yielding times of the oil. Too much water and heat could reduce the quality, and if mixed longer than the usual time, it could decrease the life of the oil. Finally, the paste, oil, and water can be separated through centrifugation. After the tedious process, the oil has been pressed and ready for display.

Believers in Christ are figuratively like the making of the olive oil. Once we accept the commitment of entering God's harvest, we are handpicked in seasons to go through the crushing process. I can speak for myself of having gone through seasons that required things, natures, ways, and old habits to be pressed out of my life. There was cleansing and stripping, like the olive at the beginning of the crushing process. The olives were cleansed off, and after that, they were ready for the crushing. The crushing shreds off the flesh so the oil can be released. 2 Corinthians 5:17 says, "Therefore, if anyone is in Christ, he is a new creation; old things have passed away; behold, all things have become new." When we come into Christ, we come with old natures. We have confessed our sinful nature, but that does not mean we have fully overcome our flesh. There must be a separation between soul and spirit. We are made up of three parts, spirit, soul, and body. The body is separate from the soul, so the soul is separated from the spirit. Hebrews 4:12 says, "For the word of God is living and operative and sharper than any two-edged sword and piercing even to the dividing of **soul** and **spirit** and of joints and marrow, and able to discern the thoughts and intentions of the heart."

Our spirit is our inner-being which God communicates with regularly. When we have those moments and say things like, "Something told me," That something may very well be the voice of God. We hear God speaking to our spirit, and sometimes we yield, and there are other times we discard it for various reasons. The soulish part of us is our mind, will, and emotions. This part of us is usually led or instructed by either our flesh or God. In Luke 1:46-47, Mary said, "My soul magnifies the Lord, and my spirit has rejoiced in God my Savior." Her spirit directed her soul to give praises to God. The soulish nature can either work for us or against us. And the body is our earthly clothing, the realm by which we feel, taste, touch, see, and hear. This part of us expresses our inner-man, spirit-led or flesh-led. The believer's crushing process is preparing for a magnificent work, the oil that is within. We must be separated from our sinful nature daily. The oil that is within us will not produce properly without crushing. Every new season requires new ways of thinking, new vision, strategies, and a new ideology. Jesus made all things new (Revelations 21:5) after His crushing. He endured the crushing process on the cross for the sake of all humankind that our sins would be forgiven through the shedding of His blood. Once He separated from the flesh, He left an exceptional quality of oil that would last a lifetime for those receiving Him (Holy Ghost).

Israel's wilderness was their crushing. After a long hard journey in bondage, they needed physical deliverance, moral deliverance, and spiritual deliverance. They needed therapy, but they were not open to the new because of the limits they had on God. It was difficult for them to trust the crushing process. God wanted to bring them into their new, but they continued to focus on the old, how they once had it and what they had.

Jesus said it best, "You cannot pour new wine in old wineskins" (Matthew 9:14-17). Jesus was responding to a question of one of the disciples of John the Baptist about fasting. They asked why His disciples did not fast like everyone else. In verse fifteen, Jesus was implying that there was no need for His disciples to fast because He was still with them. It was not yet time for fasting, and they had no reason to fast. Fasting is a symbol of mourning. John the Baptist's preaching focused on law, and his message was strong. The people measured themselves to the law and saw how they came up short every day. Jesus' message, however, was focused on life, having victory over sinful nature, and being reconciled back to God. Jesus is the new wine, and the law is the old wineskin. He did not come to repair the law but to bring something new.

What is God making in you? Have you asked God for your purpose? If so, are you listening and waiting for His response? Is your focus on the law/religion or Christ?

EXAMINING THE HEART'S POSTURE

"Jesus replied, 'You must love the Lord your God with all your heart, all your soul, and all your mind'" (Matthew 22:37).

In every wilderness season, it is a suitable time to examine yourself. It is a time to self-reflect and look within. Doing so will help you understand who you are and why you do what you do when times are good or bad. We must have the love of God in our hearts to endure hardship and uncertainties. Having good works and no love is like sounding brass and clanging symbols (1 Corinthians 13:1). In other words, Paul is saying you are just making a bunch of noise. Your labor, in fact, is in vain. If we have love, we have loyalty. Daniel showed loyalty to God in his wilderness. Daniel's period of exile was his wilderness season. The Babylonians took him from his land to serve in a foreign land under a wicked leader (read the Book of Daniel). Even though Daniel was in a place he did not desire to be in, he did not withhold his godly abilities. What I mean by that is that he did not allow the current uncertainties of being a prisoner in a foreign land to stop his loyalty and daily devotion to God. He continued to trust and believe God in a foreign place. When God interrupts our normal and brings us into a place of uncertainties, our trust in Him will depend on how well we get through a season of uncertainties and how well we function.

Daniel was young when he went into captivity. He was incredibly wise for his age, and he captured the attention of many. He was a modern-day messenger of God. He had the gift of prophecy and interpretation. Daniel knew God's most private thoughts as they were revealed to him. He showed a great deal of conviction when his faith was evaluated, and he earned long-term respect. A heart committed to God will possess the favor and abilities to know beyond the finite mind. Deuteronomy 29:29 says, "The secret things belong to our God, but those things which are revealed belong to us and to our children forever, that we may do all the words of the law." Daniel's committed heart earned him a place with God, and he knew the secret things of God. God does not reveal everything to us as we are finite, limited, and immature. We do not fully understand the infinite nature of God as we cannot know everything He does, but the word of God has been revealed to us. We have been saved by the grace of Jesus Christ and have relevant examples and principles for all generations forever.

Our commitment to God can cause others to worship Him. Daniel's commitment to God causes a wicked king like Nebuchadnezzar to fall to his face and worship him after Daniel interpreted a dream God revealed to him. He also promoted Daniel to a prominent position in his cabinet. The heart must be postured properly towards God in a wilderness and outside of a wilderness season. Our growth depends on it, the effectiveness of our gifts and works, and the lives around us depend on it. The heart must be disciplined first to love God in all purity, and the wilderness comes to discipline the heart by stripping it from all its idols and distractions. Times of uncertainties will reveal what the heart possesses; therefore, quieting the heart during such times is necessary to the believer who desires to grow in God.

God wants to use us as He did Daniel. We should be consecrated enough before Him that He would use us in the darkest places to bring light. Daniel was not interested in power for personal glory, which reminds us of Jesus. Jesus did not come to make a reputation for Himself, but He humbled Himself and became a slave, and He was exalted (Philippians 2:7-8 and Matthew 23:12). Daniel was a type-shadow of Jesus Christ. He had a heart committed to doing God's work, and he was exalted in his place of uncertainties. The heart in the wilderness must be unwavering and settled on what God is doing in that moment and what He desires life to be like when this is all said and done.

OBEDIENCE IS KEY

"But Samuel replied, 'What is more pleasing to the Lord, your burnt offerings and sacrifices or your obedience to his voice? Listen! Obedience is better than sacrifices, and submission is better than offering the fat of rams" (1 Samuel 15:22).

A key is pivotal to anything in life. It gives us the necessary access. A key can regulate music and be regarded as a function or an important person essential to a culture. Jesus is the key to everlasting life. The more I walked with the Lord I had to learn obedience. Obeying God demonstrates the faith we develop in Him.

We learned to obey in our youth. If we were raised in the right environment, obedience was important if we wanted something or to be looked upon as favorable. It was a sign of a well-mannered child that everyone loved. God had good reasons and intentions in Ephesians 6:1, when Paul said, "Children, obey your parents in the Lord, for it is right." Why is it right to obey at a young age? And what if your parents are not in the Lord? Does that child still obey their parents? It's right for parents to teach obedience whether they are of the Lord or not. If the parent teaches sound principles, it will guide the child properly to live successfully. Of course, the success is defined by what one considers success; however, it is always right to properly guide your child through life. Being a parent of God, we properly guide our children in the Lord because we belong to Him. So, we guide by the principles of God and our common knowledge of life. It is right to obey in youth as it leads to wisdom. Therefore, it is right. Godly parents are a representation of God. Accepting their guidance produces wisdom and self-discipline. It is one of the greatest teachers a parent should pass on to a child. If a child wants to be wise in life, listening to a parent and doing as they say, they find help. The principle of obedience also applies to the adult believer, also known as a child of God. We are like children in the eyes of God. Why? He is Abba Father, the parent and guardian of believers everywhere. Metaphorically, we are children, and therefore, we must obey Him to obtain the wisdom of life and develop a life of self-discipline. As a parent helps a child who listens, so much will God also provide help for those who obey and follow His principles. Obedience to God is developed when we become familiar with His written word and spend personal time with Him. A child will never know a parent if the parent never spends time with the child, as we will never know God if we do not spend enough time with Him. Getting to know God through His Word does not necessarily mean following all the Old Testament customs and practices, as those times called for such practices to discipline them to walk before God. However, by studying the Old Testament, you learn of God's character and how He loves, His impeccable patience with such fickle children (Israel & Judah). You learn how to love like God. If you truly pay attention to the writer's expression of those times, you will learn a lot about God's character.

In 1 Samuel 15:22, Samuel the prophet delivered a message to Saul because of his disobedience to God. Saul had one job, and that was to destroy all the Amalekites and all their possessions, but instead, Saul's self-righteousness got the best of him. He decides to spare the life of the king of the Amalekites and the best of all his possessions (verse 8). He only destroyed what he felt was worthless. Saul had done a horrible thing; however, he was so prideful that he did not recognize his sin before God. Saul thought he was victorious over the Amalekites, but he had failed dramatically because of his disobedience. Saul sounds much like us today. Too often, believers miss God because our freedom to make decisions seems so right, and the greatest moments can feel like a victory, but instead, it is an epic failure, all because of disobedience. Churches today were established out of disobedience, but because the intentions are to bring glory to God, the concept blinds the actions, and we miss God.

Two things please God, faith (Hebrews 11:6) and obedience. It is impossible to please God without the two in every believer's life. Faith and obedience place us under an open heaven. This is a form of submission to God. In verse 15, when Samuel chastised Saul for his disobedience, he said, "Obedience is better than a sacrifice, and submission is better than offering the fat of rams." In churches today, this passage is often used to provoke members to pay their tithes and offering, but I beg to differ. Tithing and offering today are parallel to the ox, rams, lambs, and sheep in the days of old. These offerings are symbolic of having faith that God will honor the sacrifice. But Samuel said, "Obedience is far better than a sacrifice." God does not honor obedience and sacrifices the same, but one has more weight than the other. A sacrifice is to surrender something to pay homage to or a symbol of devotion. Now Saul did not obey God, but he kept Agag's possessions that he would be able to offer what he stole up to God as a sacrifice. Obedience is a form of submission. Saul did not submit to God's directions, and therefore, God regretted establishing him as king (verse 10). His sacrifice was not good enough, yet it was evil.

The last thing any believer would want is God to have regrets and become rejected because of failing to obey Him. Today, most members are deceived into thinking their tithes and offering will get them closer to God, but it does not. God is not interested in earthly possessions. Colossians 3:2 says, "Set your affections on the things above, not the things of the earth." Obedience and submission to God are vital, and our lives depend on them.

LOSE CONTROL

"Lose Control" I heard the Spirit of God say this phrase to me during my wilderness season in 2017. This phrase was a bit controversial when I heard it. It insinuated such a weakness that I could not imagine just doing it on my own. What I mean is, I took this phrase as if God wanted me to go off the hinges. You hear a phrase like this when someone loses their mind or bodily fluids. I thought He was asking me to have a mental breakdown, so I asked Him, "Lord, why do you want me to lose my sanity?" He remained quiet. He allowed me to ponder on the phrase until I was ready to hear its meaning. I got it about two days later.

Certainly, God is not the author of confusion but wisdom and clarity. He chooses to use the foolish things of this world to confound the wise. He uses what the world would consider weak to bring shame to the powerful (1 Corinthians 1:27). This phrase certainly sounds foolish to ask someone to do, but there is so much wisdom tied to it that it brought me to another level with God and in my faith.

I could not rest with this phrase in my head, "lose control." I did not ask anyone to help me to interpret it because I really felt foolish for hearing it, but days later is when it hit me. On the evening of February 20, 2017, during the first prayer watch of the day (6 pm-9 pm), I began to reflect as I sat quietly still pondering. What I discovered in my heart was hurt. I was hurting because I always rushed to a conclusion or rested on my desires. I realized that I could be a bit unreasonable with the process of things if it did not go my way, and I expected things to happen in my timing.

My behaviors hurt me. I did not realize how unreasonable I was. I did not realize how little faith I had in God in my overall life, but what I did realize is that this phrase was a call to sacrifice. It was another level of faith. Now I get it, lose control of your will, lose control of your plans, how you see things, and want things to pan out. Lose control and render it to God that I would be able to attain His wisdom for any situation.

Being an independent single parent for eighteen years, I developed a sense of self-sufficiency that I can make things happen when and how I want. As the head of the household, everything goes your way. I had been in this pattern of life for so long that I did not realize it was hindering my devotion to God.

God wanted to discipline me with these two words, "lose control." He will use whatever is necessary to get us to learn of Him. It is quite common when we are entering a new season, culture, or environment. We become so controlled by ourselves that we attempt to become wise in our own eyes. Not knowing what to expect, our biases and prejudices start to get the best of us, and before you know it, we are no longer open to what the new can bring or how it can even enlighten us for the next.

I recently experienced this at a high school graduation I attended for one of my clients. This young lady had just completed a significant milestone in her life, and she had no family members there to support her accomplishment, so I tagged along with her. She graduated from an alternative school in the inner city of Milwaukee. Of course, with the new normal, the ceremony was not like other graduations I have attended in the past. COVID-19 forced extreme changes on everything. They had about twelve graduates, and no one could enter the building until authorized by personnel to prevent the spread of this virus. Cars were pulling up to the school, people were getting rowdy with excitement, and there were no directives. So, it happened; my controlled self kicked in, along with my biases and prejudices. Immediately, I begin to complain while sitting in the car with my client.

Neither one of us knew what was happening or what to expect, so she agreed with my murmuring. At this point, all I wanted to do was just leave (control). We both were thinking the same thing, just hand us the diploma, and we can go (control). Thank God we outlasted the unknown, and we stayed. They began to hand out sticky notes with a number on them. Then things began to make sense, so now we know they are calling the graduates in by these numbers one at a time. We wait! Thank heaven she was number four. When her number was called, we were welcomed into the building by personnel. We walked into the vestibule where there were cheering-masked faculties, a cameraman, backdrops, and a cap and gown dressing area. They had the vestibule decorated so eloquently with 2020 balloons and bouquets. It was immaculate. The school had done a fantastic job expressing their solidary of the students' achievements. They took pictures and more pictures as they screamed and waved at her. I was overjoyed by being there with her. It was an overall wonderful experience.

Once all twelve students received their commencements, the school set up and catered a nice meal and cake for the graduates and their guests and served it outside, still hot and prepackaged. They had it all together.

It was so nice that I had to repent to my client for my complaining because it should never have happened. Every day, I am still learning to lose control. This is an important disciplinary skill we must be open to as we walk with Christ. Everything and all things will not go our way. When God is bringing us into the new, we should not have our own expectations or interpretation of how things should be, but we consult with God and ask for His wisdom and patience with the process. Losing control is having a sense of discipline and surrendering all control to God the Father in heaven. Do not judge what you do not understand, do not leave what you do not know, and do not bring your unsolicited biases/opinion, but wait on the Lord, and He will lead, guide, reveal and direct in time.

We need self-control (Galatians 5) while living in this world so that we are not living to satisfy our flesh (sinful nature). This is another discipline we must possess to become single-minded with Christ.

The Israelites needed to lose control in their wilderness. They had been in a controlled environment under a wicked king for forty years. It was hard for them not to want what they once had in Egypt and not bring that mindset when God delivered them. The Israelites obviously could not see what God was trying to do. They did not know He opened a world of opportunity and a different hope. It took them four hundred years to get there.

STAY IN COMMUNION WITH GOD

The unknown can indeed throw you completely off your game if you are not careful. As I mentioned in the previous chapter, systematic thinking can get in the way of transitioning or embarking on something new, making it easy to lose sight. And where there is no vision, there is a loss of momentum. Worst case scenario, your entire focus will be on you and not on God and what He is doing. We always need momentum. Especially during a transition, times like this require us to be the driving forces of the plan.

Before God changed Abram's name to Abraham, he was quite vigilant about the unknown. In Genesis 12, both God and Abram were faithful to each other. In verse one, God began to work His plan here on the earth. He came to Abram with hard instructions and prerequisites for His plan. Abram had to obey (the key) God to obtain the blessings mentioned in verse two. He had to leave what was familiar to him and go where things were unfamiliar. Any unknown place can be considered a wilderness. Abram's wilderness began with a conversation between him and God. My wilderness season began with a dream which led to a conversation with God. The Spirit of God gave me consolation through Abram's life when I had to take that leap of faith. My leaders had become like parents to me, and I, too, had to leave my father's house and go to a place that I did not know. And because I did not know, I made every effort to remain watchful for danger and clarity.

In verse two, Abram did what any faithful believer would do; without question, he departed. Here is what was an interesting lesson I learned on the journey. Throughout Abram's journey, the conversation between him and God never ceased. This is how we keep focus during the unknown by "staying in communion with God." I built an altar in my prayer room that had these words posted over it as a reminder because, along the way, it is easy to forget that God started the journey. Abram listened and worshipped God and God was able to invoke and guide him. He was able to remain vigilant and selfless during the journey. Abraham was considered "The Father of Faith." He believed God with the unknown, and it was counted to him as righteousness (Romans 4:1-3). He was justified by faith and faith alone and not by works. This is required of us today. Being vigilant is having faith in God and His plan. Trusting in God acknowledges that He does know all things, and you trust what He knows. Like Abraham, we should not allow our unbelief to get in the way of God's plan for our lives, never wavering but being fully convinced that what He promised He is also able to perform (Romans 4:20-21).

Keeping your vigilance in transition will bring confidence and courage to continue even when you do not have all the details. While you are watchful for God's details, your focus is less on you and more on the work that lies ahead. It will not matter what others may think or say about your decision because what they do not know is that you have decided to follow the Spirit of Christ for your life and no longer man-made traditions, the familiar.

Chapter Four

THE DANGER OF COMPLACENCY

Complacency is the enemy of growth, just like comfort. This level is called a plateau. This level causes one to remain stable, preventing one from rising beyond that level or progressing forward. This place is much like an addiction. Once you open your heart and mind to it, it is hard to kick the habit and find your footing again. It is pure deception. It is a feeling of quiet pleasure or security, often while unaware of potential danger or defect. It is a place of self-satisfaction with an existing situation or condition. We have all been in a place like this, and it is not a safe place to be in.

I am reminded of Luke 22:46 when Jesus went to the Mount of Olives to pray. He took three of His disciples with Him to intercede for Him. He left them with instructions to watch and pray while He went a little further to pray. Jesus was about ready to fulfill His purpose on the earth. He was getting ready to experience the worst pain ever inflicted on man, knowing His Father in heaven would turn His back on Him. So, He was serious as He prayed. After encountering heavy prayer, He came back to find the disciples sleeping. The disciples had been overtaken by sleep. Sleep can be like kryptonite to your prayer life. It can seriously weaken your prayer life and cause harm if you allow sleep to abandon your prayer time. Though kryptonite is a fictional word in the entertainment world, its context has relevance to a life devoted to prayer. The disciples were weakened by their kryptonite. What they experienced is no different from what we experience today. When the Spirit of God pulls on us to pray at the wee hours of the night, we cannot keep our eyes open long enough to even ask Him for direction in prayer. We would rather find comfort in sleep than be in an uncomfortable position (on our knees) in prayer. Jesus gave a fair warning of what will happen if you do not pray at the appointed time. He told the disciples in verse forty, "Pray that they will not give in to temptation." He gave them sound counsel on what could happen if they abandoned their duty to pray.

There is a phrase most used within this new generation, "Stay woke." From artists to activists, this is a prevalent term used within the Black communities to bring about social awareness. It is to make sure the people are aware of our community's current realities. Stay woke is a watch term and can also become prevalent during watch hours through the night. This time of alertness can bring such an awareness of the season given only by the Holy Spirit.

Sleeping is evidence of what complacency looks like. We lose the battle by actual sleep, and we merit ourselves for doing absolutely nothing. This is complacency with your eyes wide open while the mind and body produce nothing. When we sleep, we feel safe and comfortable. It brings self-pleasure, and it is hard to let it go. Believers intentionally doing nothing are in a state of complacency, and in that state, there is a similar sense of comfort as if one were sleeping. There are no expectations to grow. They are not being challenged to go deeper with God. During this time, people like this spend more time pleasing themselves through materialism, emotionalism, or other unhealthy habits birthed through sin. The complacent believer can become extremely vulnerable to their surroundings. Just as anything can happen to us during actual sleep, it is the same principle if we sleep with our eyes wide open. Rest with our eyes wide open is often orchestrated by ourselves, and we become complacent to the will of God. We put ourselves in a dangerous position and easily become vulnerable to sin.

Is this the temptation Jesus was referring to when He warned the disciples? How can they be tempted in their sleep? Satan is always lurking like a lion seeking who he can destroy (1 Peter 5:8). Sleeping is a crevice for the enemy to come in and tempt the mind. Therefore, the disciples made it relatively easy for Satan to entice them through a dream or even something coming upon them unaware. Too much sleep or a lack of productivity brings about laziness, and a lazy vessel is more susceptible/vulnerable to sin. We must keep our minds set on pleasing God and not ourselves. In Philippians 2:5, Paul counseled the Philippians, "Let this mind be in you which was also in Christ Jesus." Every day Jesus took on the mind of His Father so that He might know His will (John 6:38). Jesus is the greatest example of how to live a life pleasing to God, and today believers everywhere must decide to serve themselves in the flesh, serve man through tradition, or serve God in faith. All of these require giving up something, but only one of them will lead you to eternal life. We must be cautious not to allow complacency to influence our wilderness journey, stay alert, and keep watch as well as pray.

THE LUST OF FLESH, THE LUST OF THE EYE AND THE PRIDE OF LIFE

"For all that is in the world, the lust of the flesh, the lust of the eye and the pride of life, is not of the Father, but of the world." (1 John 2:16)

This passage is why we must be watchful every wakening moment of our lives. John tells of the three realms of sin operating in the world we live in; these very sins are ready to influence us daily. Knowing this, Paul said in Romans 12:2 (I love the way the NLT puts it), "Don't copy the behavior and customs of this world, but let God transform you into a new person by changing the way you think. Then you will learn to know God's will for you, which is good and pleasing and perfect." We easily succumb to these three areas of temptation unknowingly because the mind has not been renewed. Paul said to let God transform our minds. The only way to successfully let God transform our mind is with a willingness to surrender it to Him, acknowledging we are imperfect and we need Him. This is the point of losing complete utter control. Instead, it is these areas of sin that stagnate the believers today. They are the very reason we do not know the will of God for our lives and easily become a ship without a sail, simply going with the winds and waves of the world.

- **The lust of the flesh** is what the world offers through physical cravings, mainly exploited through the media, i.e., materialism, socialism, fame, or any other form of aggrandizing.
- **The lust of the eye** is wanting everything we see. This is a self-centered nature; I can get anything I want and refuse to control inner cravings and deny my desires.
- And lastly, **the pride of life** is the achiever or the possessor; when you are more driven and impressed by your goals, accomplishments, and personal ambitions.

We have missed that Satan tempted Jesus in all three manners of sin. In Matthew 4, the Holy Spirit led Jesus into the wilderness to be tempted by Satan. Jesus had to be tempted this way to fulfill the power of resisting the devil. Jesus was subjected to the same weaknesses that we experience today. Yet He was God in the form of flesh; the fleshly clothing made Him just like humankind. God is the Spirit, and Jesus being Him in the flesh, He now feels what we feel through His Son. After fasting for forty days and forty nights, in verse three, the tempter came and said, "If You are the Son of God, command that these stones become bread" **(the lust of the**

flesh). This was a perfect time for Jesus to satisfy His hunger after fasting for so long. He had the power to turn whatever He wanted into any type of nourishment to fulfill His hunger. But His response was of loyalty to His Father. Jesus replied, "It is written, Man shall not live by bread alone, but by every word that proceeds from the mouth of God." Have you ever been defeated during or after a fast the Lord called you on?

Satan was not done; he is and always will be relentless when we are weak in the flesh. In verse five, he took Jesus up to the pinnacle of Jerusalem and said to Him, "If You are the Son of God, throw Yourself down. For it is written: 'He shall give His angels charge over you,' and in their hands they shall bear you up, lest you dash your foot against a stone.'" **(The pride of life)**, here Jesus being God in the form of flesh, He could have highly esteemed Himself in having the power to take up His own life if He fell or called on the angels to aid Him. Jesus showed this same humility on the cross (He could have called ten thousand angels, Matthew 26:53), but instead, Jesus replied, "It is written again, you shall not tempt the Lord your God." Jesus quotes the Holy Scriptures.

And the last test is in verses eight and nine. Satan once again takes Jesus to a high mountain and shows Him the kingdoms of the world and its glory, and he says, "All these things I will give You if You fall down and worship me." **(The lust of the eye)** He wanted to pursue Jesus through what He saw. Satan could not have believed that Jesus was so weak in His flesh and He would look for satisfaction in the world. Furthermore, what Satan showed Jesus had already belonged to Him (Hebrews 2:10-18). You cannot give something to someone that is already theirs. Jesus' final response, yet again, He quotes the Holy Scripture, but this time with an intensity of emotion or loudness. Jesus replied, "Away with you, Satan! For it is written, 'You shall not worship the Lord your God, and Him only you shall serve.'"

We learn from Jesus' temptation not to give in so easily to Satan's foolish offers. Jesus rebuked Satan, not in His own might, but in the might of the scriptures. Yes, He was the word in flesh form, but we must remember that being in the flesh did not exempt Him from our day-to-day struggles. He was wrapped in imperfection, yet He was able to resist Satan. Jesus had in mind to please the Father by fulfilling His will here on earth. We have this same commission today in our lives. The word of God must be engraved on our hearts to keep us from falling away from Him in sin.

Satan used these same temptations with Eve in the Garden of Eden. His tactics are still the same today; they have not changed. Genesis 3:6 says, "So when the woman saw that the tree was good for food **(lust of the flesh),** that it was pleasant to the eyes **(lust of the eyes)**, and a tree desirable to make one wise **(the pride of life)**, she took of its fruit and ate. She also gave to her husband with her, and he ate." Here it is true that a woman can be a man's worst downfall. Certainly, Adam should have known better, considering God gave him the instruction and not Eve (Genesis 2:17). Surely, we can say, disobeying God and listening to man is any believer's worst downfall. The scriptures give us wisdom and power to resist Satan in our flesh. Though there is no perfect one but the One without sin (John 8:7), we all fall until we decide to use our liberty to do what is right in the sight of God.

WARNING AGAINST SELF-LOATHING

Self-loathing is another enemy of progress; it is the opposition to love. God has called us to hate sin and not ourselves. We must understand that self-hatred stems from underlying issues, i.e., not feeling attractive, guilty conscience, feeling bad all the time, lack of accomplishments, or being wrongfully treated at a time in life. All of which lie underneath the surface of our lives, unidentified and unspoken. Believers in Christ battle with self-hatred as we are not immune to it. This is a common struggle, and we must know that we are not alone. We have the Word of God to ensure us that God's thoughts towards us are good and not thoughts of evil (Jeremiah 29:11). Evil thoughts do not come by way of the Holy Spirit but

Satan himself. He loves self-hatred as it is his fuel to cause self-destruction. But God's thoughts of us cause hope. In times of self-loathing, we must remember the finished work of Christ at Calvary, that He is willing and able to deliver us from this body of death (Romans 7:23-24).

A wilderness season can only be as impactful as you allow it to be. This time of solitude with God is a time to reflect and, as I mentioned before, a time to listen. Be incredibly careful during this time, as self-loathing can creep into the mind. God enforces us to look again, but this time from within. We have relied on our accomplishments and appearances to complete us for far too long, but there is little productivity, no props, and not much human contact in the wilderness. God uses a wilderness to get our attention which means what we used to use as our makeup or sense of being is no longer accessible to us. If you take away a person's pedigree or position, this could cause negative thoughts to surface. It may even cause those unspoken issues to resurface in a bad way. We must be ready to confront these negative thoughts with the Word of God so that we remain hopeful in Him. When you refuse to adapt, adjust, and embrace the time of discipline a wilderness brings, your thoughts of hope could dry up very quickly. Before you know it, you can become a complainer and/or doubter of all things pertaining to God, and you lack the understanding that self-hatred is a sin.

WARNING AGAINST SECRET SIN

"People who conceal their sins will not prosper, but if they confess and turn from them, they will receive mercy" (Proverbs 28:13). Secret sin is another growth stunter. A stunted person cannot grow or be adequately developed when something is there, hindering the process. As a tree needs water to grow, it withers away and eventually dies without it, like our spiritual lives when we do not value the mercy of God as we would water. We are like trees, and mercy is like water. We need the mercy of God to redeem, cleanse and wash us from our sins daily. However, it depends on how you view or value mercy. A dehydrated person would value a glass of water, considering it a perfect gift. Why? Because the body becomes fatigued and unable to function correctly when it is deprived of such substance. God's mercy is like a substance. In fact, once received, it gives us substance and morality. It is just as necessary to our walk as water is to our bodies. His mercy is a gift He presented through His Son, Jesus Christ. Until it is recognized as such, we will not fully enjoy it or ask for it when we need it. Mercy is no different from accepting or asking for a monetary or materialistic gift. We freely ask and receive such gifts from others and sometimes create wish lists for certain occasions requesting a particular gift(s). We recognize the value in things enough to ask for them when we think we need or want them. This approach is also befitting when it comes to God's mercy. What happens when we receive a monetary or material gift? It adds to us in a unique form or fashion. It may boost our self-esteem, or it may also make us look better. For example, you may ask for a particular book, which will make you a bit more knowledgeable in that area. Well, God's mercy is intended to do that (add to you) and so much more. Mercy is much more valuable than anything on this earth. Jesus brought God's mercy through His great sacrifice for us. Because of His blood-shedding, we have been forgiven for all our sins. We receive God's compassion and forbearance when we offend Him with our actions. Mercy restores the sinful man back to God. This adds to us. It adds blessings, indescribable wealth (Proverbs 10:22), favor, peace, joy, etc. (Galatians 5:21).

David's conspiracy was a secret sin. In 2 Samuel 11:12, David conspires against Uriah, Bathsheba, and anyone impacted by his act. A conspiracy usually involves two or three persons against another. You can almost say Joab was aiding and abetting the situation. He assisted David with this conspiracy. However, a third person was also involved, which was another aspect of David, his alter ego. David did what was right in his own eyes, and 2 Samuel 11:27 says, "It displeased the Lord." God, of course, was watching the whole time, as He is today.

David is in trouble, and he thought he got away with his cruel acts by covering up. What was he thinking? David thought that God would overlook his actions because he was king, but no; instead, he is held to greater accountability due to his kingship. God required one thing from David: to follow all His commands. David had one job, and that was to be king. David may have used his position of power to sleep with the beautiful Bathsheba, and from that one decision came lies to cover up other lies. The worst is Uriah, Bathsheba's husband, carried the very letter to Joab that would mark his death. This conspiracy was so awful and heartless that innocent men died, including the child he conceived with Bathsheba. This was David's judgment from God, his punishment, and permanent consequence. He lost his wives and had to live with what he did with the sword in his home that killed Uriah. God had to send Nathan the prophet to reveal David's actions in a parable, and Nathan also delivered his consequence. It was funny how David was ready to kill the man Nathan mentioned in the parable. He had no idea that the man was him until Nathan revealed to David that God had seen what he had done, and He was not happy with him. It was then that David repented. He acknowledged his sin and made his confession in chapter 12. David tried it just like we all do, but unrepented sin can cause lifelong consequences and may not end well. However, when we repent, it redeems us and brings us back to a secret place with God. David continued to be king after that. Because of his confession, he still reigned. Not only that, while consoling his wife, Bathsheba, they conceived another son who was Solomon. God restored them both by giving them a son, not only a son but one who would be king over Israel. This son would build the temple back for God. Chapter 12:24 says, "Now the Lord loved him (Solomon)."

God did not count David out because of his actions, so much so that Jesus would even come from the lineage of David. So, when we confess and forsake our sins, it is not only for us but for generations to come. It is for God to bless the entire bloodline so that the inheritance can flow. No repentance and hiding our sins will only corrupt the generations, leaving them to fend for themselves and bring judgment against our soul. So many times, we mess up and count ourselves as unworthy or unredeemable as if God is not able or unwilling. If God can bring David back from such an awful experience, what will He not do for us when we fall short. David is no greater than us. God has no respect of a person. He is always ready to forgive us if we are willing to confess and forsake our sins to Him.

I love the NLT version of 1 Corinthian 10:13, "The temptation in your life is no different from what others experience. And God is faithful. He will not allow the temptation to be more than you can stand. When you are tempted, He will show you a way out so that you can endure." God used Nathan, the prophet, to bring David out. Though David was cleared from his actions, it looks like he got off scot-free, and it was done; but no, he was still in his temptation because he had not dealt with it. If David had not repented, there is a chance he may have done something like this again. I mean, why not? If he got away with it once, he would likely do it again. But God made a way of escape because He loved David and had plans for his life, so David endured.

David and his victory inspire me, but one thing is for sure, I am so glad that God did not have to come down from heaven with a word of rebuke for my sinful thoughts. I am so glad He did not have to reveal it to a prophet to call me out. Because I love Him dearly and what He thinks of me is important, I immediately went to God for help. I knew I was in trouble. Daily I cried out, asking for His perfect aid. It takes a conviction in your spirit to go to God and confess you have done wrong. Sometimes we override the conviction because we want to stay in a place of sin and defeat, but when you know God has called you to a vineyard and you have hindered the calling by your actions, love draws one into a confession without a doubt. I called Him, and He answered me. Confession was my way of escape.

However, every day was still a battle. It was a struggle to keep my mind from slipping. I was so scared that I had to rely on God to take control every day. There were some days I had control, and then there were other days I did not. We do not think about the consequences when we want to satisfy our flesh. We just want what we want. I am sure this is what David felt when he first saw Bathsheba. Deep down inside, he knew it was wrong, but when no one was looking and he had the authority to orchestrate her being brought to him, David went for it. If you can see yourself in David, then you know it is hard when only part of your mind is made up. In other words, we become particle, wayward, and double-minded. James 1:8 says, "A double-minded man is unstable in all his ways." God meant it when He inspired this passage. The verse before this says, "Let not that man suppose that he will receive anything from the Lord." We have nothing coming from the Lord if we simultaneously pray, ask, and doubt. We must believe that He can do it if we want to receive. It is knowing that God can do it, what the problem is, and whether we will let Him do it or continue to be wise in our own eyes like David?

Solomon was David's son, born through his conspiracy. He was full of wisdom. Why? Because he recognized he needed the wisdom to rule his kingdom. Though he did not ask for it in a timely manner to properly function in it, God still gifted him with nobility, even with his mistakes. His wisdom was so inevitable that Queen Bathsheba traveled to Jerusalem to experience it (1 Kings 10:1-7).

Solomon had enough sin in his life that he knew how ineffective he could become when it was not confronted. Israel was instructed not to take a wife from foreign nations, and here Solomon took seven hundred wives and princesses and three hundred concubines, which caused him to turn his heart away from God. He became utterly ineffective, and it jeopardized his kingship. In 1 Kings 11:9-13, Solomon angered God, and He took the kingdom away from him. The results of Solomon's sins were inevitable, but the evitable was lust. He had such a weakness for women that he lost himself.

Unconfessed sins can cost you everything. Pride causes us to conceal our sins. It is an attempt to avoid being looked at differently, frowned upon, or excommunicated from a group or organization. Are you like Solomon?

You simply cannot resist the flesh. Solomon took pride in choosing wives for his pleasure. Solomon used his freedom asking to satisfy his flesh. Galatians 5:13 tells us, "For you, brethren, have been called to liberty, only do not use liberty as an opportunity for the flesh, but through love serve one another." You can be tempted to do as you please during a wilderness season. Not knowing the direction or where the next provision will come from, it is quite easy to lose sight of why God has called one to such a challenging place. In the wilderness, we must be willing to search ourselves for any manners of sin, confess them, practice them no more, and surely receive God's mercy. He remembers our faults no more and counts us worthy again.

Chapter Five

NO OTHER GODS

"You shall have no other gods before Me" (Exodus 20:3). You will know when idols are present in your life. You will know when you are entertaining something other than your God-given calling. When idols come, they tend to take your undivided attention away from the purpose of God. Idolatry disconnects us from the presence of God to the point we lose the longing for Him. It comes from an idled place.

Idled means to do absolutely nothing, not in use or operation, not working, which is also a form of complacency (Dictionary.com, 2022). In chapter four, we talked about complacency being the enemy of growth. It is a place of not being fully aware or awake, sleeping with your eyes wide open, and in a very vulnerable state. Idle and complacency are parallel to one another. When we choose to do nothing, boredom and emptiness settle in, and we begin searching for fulfillment. We begin searching for the answer through things or people rather than God. This was Israel's position in their wilderness. This is what prohibited them from advancing out of their wilderness experience in a timely manner. The Israelites had become hardhearted and impatient with the process and decided to go their own way. They made the journey hard for themselves because they failed to continue to look to God. They passed through lands (Numbers 33) and the wildernesses before reaching the promised land, and each one had significance from which we can learn.

- ❖ ***The Wilderness of Shur*** *(Marah), which means bitter. They experienced their freedom, testing of thirst, beauty, provision, promises, and wonders in this wilderness. It was near the Red Sea because Israel had just crossed it when they came upon Marah. Though they were glad to be out of confinement, they ran into another problem; there was no water to drink. But when they came upon Marah, they found water, but it was bitter. They could not drink it lest they catch a disease and die. Israel complained to Moses, and Moses went to God and cried out for the people. God made the waters sweet through a tree branch. This was a place where bitter waters were made sweet and God's time of testing His people with promises (Exodus 15). God provided twelve springs of water and seventy palm trees.*

In our wilderness, we will experience droughts, not to harm or discourage us but to discipline us to lean on Him again and to trust Him with our lives morally.

- ❖ ***The Wilderness of Sin*** *(Between Elim and Sinai). This time their hunger was tested. They grumbled against God in their lack. Once again, Moses sought God on their behalf, and God provided manna from heaven (meat and bread). Israel's disobedience began to rise, and all of them did not follow Moses' command to gather enough for the day and not leave any leftovers. Moses knew God was going to provide fresh manna every day. In our times of lack, any little provision made, we will overstock out of fear of running out. This is not trusting God (Exodus 16).*

It is quite common that we immediately revert to our own plans and fail to ask God for help in times of testing. This wilderness specifically disciplines us to follow God's exact counsel.

- ❖ ***The Wilderness of Sinai** was a time of reflection, affirming, and preparation to meet with God, the great unveiling. In this wilderness, God revealed Himself to Israel. His presence descended, and He officialized his commands and ordinances with His people. As we continue the journey with God, He will reveal Himself to us and make His covenant known to us (Exodus 19).*

This wilderness is to discipline the mind to look at where we came from, where we are now, and prepare us for what is to come. It will benefit every believer to be open to this process and reflect on the good, bad, and ugly. Have patience with the process and wait for God to unveil the bigger picture.

- ❖ ***The Wilderness of Zin** represents rebellion, trespassing, and strategy. During this time of Israel's wandering, they were about 37 years in. Many of the elders had children and died Miriam and Aaron during this time. Israel was once again weary from the journey, still unyielding to God's plan, and they refused to listen to Moses. But not only was the journey weighing on them, but also Moses. Israel desired drink because they were thirsty, they complained to Moses. Moses did what he would typically do, seek God for provision. God instructed Moses to speak to the rock, but he hit the rock out of his frustrations. Not once, but twice. Because of his rebellion, God did not allow him to take Israel to the promised land (Numbers 20).*

Remember, there are consequences when we do not obey God's direct counsel. Hold fast to the fact that He is still speaking and guiding you in the unknown.

> ❖ ***The Wilderness of Paran*** *is where Israel was during most of their wandering, here and the* ***Wilderness of Zin****. In this wilderness, Moses' name was defamed because of his actions. There was confrontation with God, chastising, God's wrath, judgment, punishment, and intercession (Numbers 13 -16).*

It is likely to be ostracized when you stand out differently from the rest. When times are dire, people are more desperate for immediate results. Moses did not see things the way Israel saw things, as he only saw what God revealed to him. And what God revealed was so different from their reality. That made it difficult for Israel to trust God's counsel in him. We must not contend with God or leaders under God's direct counsel. God will show who His true leaders are through signs and wonders.

How many of us can say we have willingly moved from waiting on God to manifest something He promised to make things happen on our own and call it God? I think we can all say we have done this. This was Israel's position in the Wilderness of Mount Sinai. Moses had gone up to the presence of God (which is what Israel was used to him doing), but this time he took too long to come back to them. In their waiting, they became impatient and reverted to their own plan. Everybody yearns for a savior during times of testing. We must have something tangible to believe in. We begin creating something or someone to have hope in, placing it or them above God. Israel decided to create their god using tangible things. In Exodus 32, the people expressed their concern for Moses' absence and what may have happened to him. They petition Aaron to make their own god, and Aaron goes with the idea. So, they scavenged, created, and there they built the golden calf. They worshipped and made sacrifices to it. God, being omnipresent, saw their action and sent Moses back to Israel to deal with their actions. God cannot work through us when we elevate anyone or anything above Him.

In 2017 I stumbled upon a book called *No Other Gods* by Kelly Minter. This book helped me recognize idols present in my life that I was overlooking. Kelly Minter poured herself out like a drink offering on such an exigent subject of idolatry.

We learn of idols in the Old Testament as a common barrier between God and His people. Their idols were from morality and carved images to silver and gold. In those times, idols were distinctive but let us not overlook the fact that they still exist today. They simply manifested differently in today's time. Idolatry is anytime we put something or someone above God. This is a form of worship, and to worship means with a deep passion, energy, intensity, or giving yourself over to something. Our modern-day idols can come in all forms like spouses, children, jobs, careers, pedigree, TV, cell phones, social media, money, social status, or materialism. This list can go on.

We are like Israel today. The defiance still lives on. Believers everywhere are falling short as Israel did, and the common mistakes are:

- Failure to lean on God
- Lack of faith in leadership
- Personal ambition
- Discontented with God's will
- Lack of vision

These downfalls lead to one creating something to believe in other than God. In *No Other Gods*, Kelly Minter talks about having God in our lives and committing to do His will, yet we look to other things or even people to operate in His place. Anything can be an idol, even the things that are God-given and perfectly made for Him. Simply because where we put things in our lives often replaces Him. I find this to be a profound fact. I recall a close friendship I had for about seven years that took God's place so much that He interrupted the friendship for His name's sake. Our friendship was built on prayer and fellowship in Christ; however, it had become my go-to, and I could not see Him for myself. The friendship was a necessity, and it was so important to me that I did not see that it had become idolatry. My eyes became open to what the friendship had become after I was out of it. The Lord Himself showed me the error of my ways. What was necessary in this case was that I reflected on myself and not the other person. I can only control myself. Once I was out of it, I learned I had put all my energy and focus on the friendship, and the person became an idol. I looked up to her as if she was a god. She was a wise prayer warrior and a woman of the cloth. I could not see while in it because I was blinded by what I chose to inflate to function as God. Why? It was the satisfaction of having someone in my life that could tolerate me. It was fulfilling a long empty void I had been wrestling with probably since I was a little girl. Our friendship ended abruptly in 2014. God had to prove to me how imperfect we are as humans and to never put our confidence in the flesh/man (Philippians 3:1-4). Once the friendship dissolved, I believe I had passed through the Wilderness of Sinai. This was my time of reflection, affirmation, and God's unveiling plan for my life.

LOVE TO DEATH

In 2020, the Spirit of God further taught me how love could result in idolatry. Throughout my day, I would hear people say, "I love this person to death." Each time I heard it, my stomach would cringe, and I did not know why. I grew up hearing this quote, and in fact, I may have said it a time or two myself. But for whatever reason, now, when I hear it, it bothers my soul. I went to God in prayer and asked for understanding. He said, "To love someone to death means you would do anything for them, even if it costs you your life." This statement appears endearing because it replicates what Christ did on the cross at Calvary. He loved us unto death, but unto means until, meaning there is more. However, when we say it, it is final. I love you to death, and that is it. When you love a person or thing more than you love God, you are willing to abort the plan of God for your life.

Saying this is marking your life in a way that you could experience a type of death, whether it be spiritual or natural. It is risky to love ancestors or parents so much that you only see things through the lens of your elders. Even if the elders only had a portion of the truth, the twisted love for them sees no mistakes in their beliefs and actions that you practice their ways. In such a place, there is no further seeking God for the new or the current times in the world. Loving to death is a sign of idolatry. Again, Jesus loved us unto death, to live again. Therefore, death was not the destination. He rose and yet lives in us today. There is truth in life, in the life of Christ.

IDENTIFY AND RENDER YOUR IDOLS

I work as a Program Manager for a transitional housing program. In this position, I oversee adults' and teenagers' everyday life. I hear so many stories of what people have overcome or what they are trying to overcome. They realize it enough to know it is something from their past. Because I see so many different people from various levels of society, it is vital for me to never become judgmental towards them for the sake of collaborating effectively with them. I get a chance to see why they are faced with the challenges that have plagued their lives. One of the most common things I see is that they are unwilling to look within themselves and point out their flaws. I always hear, "I was treated wrong." They fell to identify their part in the matter. Instead, they turn away from the truth to any poor decisions that caused them to arrive at such times in their lives. My job is to assist them with developing the necessary skills that will help them become self-sufficient. But that can be difficult if they are unwilling to clean up their ways and views by revealing their idols.

The only way we can deal with our idols is first to identify them. Ask yourself, what are your idols? What are the plagues that keep you from advancing in life? Yes, these are challenging questions because now you are faced with a part of you that you have ignored over time. We must allow ourselves to feel the shame and guilt of the ugly truth, but do not stop at it.

Just feel it enough so that it brings conviction. Once we are convicted, then we must repent. Once we repent, then and then there is a great turning point. We move away from the very thing that has been plaguing our lives. This is a humbling process; this is when God can excel in you.

We do ourselves a disservice when we hide from our sin (idols). It is also a disservice when we do not admit that idols are present in our lives. Proverbs 28:13 says, "He who hides his sins will not prosper, but he who confesses and forsakes them shall have mercy." This scripture is calling for transparency. When we are transparent with ourselves, we can be transparent with God, and once we learn that, we can be openly transparent regardless of who is watching. God's mercy is everything to us. Mercy means a pardon from your wrong, not guilty, a benevolence instead of punishment, favor, and blessings (Dictionary.com, 2022). God is extending His mercy to all those willing to be transparent with Him by identifying any idols in and rending them today to Him so that He may begin a new trajectory of life through you.

HINDERING SPIRITS

We can expect hindering spirits to come in times of vulnerability, especially during a wilderness season. Israel had hindrances. They became closed off to God's ultimate plan. While God is testing, we must remember Ephesians 4. We must not close our minds and harden our hearts against God. A mind that is closed to God will have difficulties understanding the scriptures.

Always be alert in a wilderness season because Satan will turn your focus elsewhere every time, and you will stand to face these challenges.

- Our thoughts will begin to say, I cannot remember the Bible, nor do I understand what I have read.
- We struggle with the application of the word.

- We give in to minor interruptions by things or the people around us.
- We fall asleep while reading the word.
- Your mind begins to wander to other things.
- You find yourself reading the word but having a tough time focusing on what you read, nor does it influence your heart.
- You attempt to debate what you read, finding errors with it or disregarding the word because of its timeline.
- We feel judged by it rather than allowing it to change our lives.

These signs are evident and cannot be overlooked. You will know if Satan has put blinders up to keep you from being your best in Christ. Any time we come to a place of total commitment to God, he comes with his antics, which are the same every time. Therefore, Paul said in 2 Corinthians 2:11, "We are not ignorant of his (Satan) devices."

Satan can only find access if there is unbelief, lack of submission to God, worldly pleasures and concerns, and anything mind-altering, i.e., magic, soaking music, drugs or alcohol, alternate identities, and psychics. On our everyday journey to become more like Christ, we must rid ourselves of and avoid any of these self-indulging decisions.

Chapter Six

DISCIPLINE THE FLESH

"And lest I should be exalted above measure by the abundance of the revelation, a thorn in the flesh was given to me, a messenger of Satan to buffet me, lest I be exalted above measure. Concerning this, I pleaded with the Lord three times that it might depart from me. And he said to me, "My grace is sufficient for you, for My strength is made perfect in weakness." Therefore, I boast in my infirmities that the power of Christ may rest upon me. Therefore, I take pleasures in infirmities, in reproaches, in needs, in persecutions, in distresses for Christ's sake. For when I am weak, then I am strong (2 Corinthians 12:7-9)."

Christians use this passage to help them overcome sin or bring discipline to the flesh. It seems that when this passage is used, sin is usually present in one's life. But Paul was not talking about any present natures or acts.

Though he did not say what his thorn was, Bible scholars believe a physicality in his body prevented him from moving around the way he was used to. Paul, as we know, was a very independent man. He moved around quite frequently, allowing him to write most of the New Testament. He was used to being on the go. Whatever this thing was that was bothering him, it had slowed him down. In Galatians 4:13-14, when Paul revisited the Galatians, he reminisced about being sick when he first visited them with the Gospel (presented the Good News). They almost rejected him because of his physical condition, but eventually, they took care of him with diligence. This thing that was bothering him may have very well been in his body.

Mental afflictions can slow us down as well. Satan could have been attempting to taunt him with his past actions of killing innocent Christians before his encounter with Jesus Christ (Acts 9). Satan is the accuser of the brothers and sisters in Christ (Revelations 12:10). When he uses our past against us, that can sometimes function as a distraction that would either cause a complete stop or a slowdown in God's work. He gains access to our minds through crevices, i.e., insecurities, unforgiveness of ourselves, and other personal vulnerabilities. Either way, we do not know what Paul's thorn was, but we know that it was not in the likes of sin.

A thorn is something that wounds us, annoys us, or causes discomfort. As Paul was annoyed, he was annoyed enough to ask God to remove this thorn. Sin does not annoy us, nor is it discomforting. If it were, it would not be so easy to fall away in it, but sin is a nature that brings us comfort. Yes, it hurts us, but not physically. It hurts our growth in God. Our sinful nature may very well annoy God, but as for ourselves, if we are not spirit conscience, we are numb to our actions and feel absolutely nothing. So again, this thorn Paul refers to has nothing to do with sinful nature. It has everything to with limitations as a human being because of the current state of life. We have physical afflictions, mental afflictions, and there are developmental afflictions. These afflictions limit us on purpose, causing us to have constant contact with God, relying on Him alone and not ourselves in any form. God was evident in Paul's life, and those around him saw it. They benefited from what was on Paul's life, and Paul's thorn kept him humble. His thorn was necessary. The thorn reminds Paul and us that we can do nothing apart from God and nothing in our own strength, might, or power. Our energy, efforts, gifts, and talents are not enough. We need the Spirit of God to work in us to do His work effectively.

Once God spoke back to Paul's request to remove the thorn from his flesh with, "My grace is sufficient for you," Paul's demeanor completely changed. His worship changed; he became humble enough to continue as he was, and we did not read about this thorn anymore. Paul said, knowing this, I prefer to boast in my weakness (2 Corinthians 12:9). If the thorn is referred to as sin, then that means we boast in our sinful nature, are proud to be sinners, or speak with excessive vanity? I think not. We know in our subconscious and are mindful daily that we are sinners working to stay saved, but we do not keep our sinful nature before us because Christ has taken them away upon repentance. Where we have failed is the recurring sin after acknowledgment.

Repentance means to turn away from. If sin is reoccurring, it is because it is either unrepentant sin or the gesture of, "I'm sorry, I have sinned." I am sorry, only acknowledges you have done something wrong and feel bad for it, but it does not ensure that you will no longer practice the act. So, we must separate this thorn from our sinful nature as the two are not parallel. This thorn is a lack of something we feel we need to complete us to get things done. The more we remind ourselves of these weaknesses, the deeper we go in worshipping God. Our worship expresses gratitude and appreciation to Him for what He has done and what we do not have. We boast in our weaknesses by acknowledging them but not resting in them as though they are in control. They are not. God is. Once we admit our weaknesses, we simply allow God's strength to activate in our lives. And this principle goes for any manner of weakness: moral, physical, developmental, or mental.

- What are your limitations?
- Do you allow God to work through you with these limits?

During my wilderness period in 2018, there was a season of temptation that I struggled with (chapter 6). During this season, it taught me a different level of grace. God's grace, as we know, is available to us to bring about evident change, whether tangible or intangible. Grace is His favor to get satisfactory results when we do not deserve it (unmerited). We get credit instead of discredit. That is His grace. When we ask God to apply His grace to our lives, our sin is overlooked. He does not reward us according to our actions, but His grace continues to flow in our lives. This is the dispensation of Grace where it is more than enough. Still, I learned in my season of temptation that God's grace not only produces good when we do wrong, meaning after the fall, His grace picks us back up, but His grace also will keep you from falling, according to Jude 24, "Now to Him who is able to keep you from stumbling and to present you faultless before the presence of His glory with exceeding joy." I fought hard and long during this time to keep my sanity. I had journeyed alone for a period and fell weak to my flesh. Every day I would intensify my prayers to keep me from self-destructing, and His grace kept me. His grace saved me from myself. His grace will get us through without compromise. Too much emphasis on His grace only bringing us back from our sins can distract us from the reality that His grace can also keep us from sin, that we will remain faultless in God's sight.

MY CONFESSION

My wilderness journey began on February 28, 2017. The first year I was strong in the Lord because of my seeking and hunger to understand why He called me out of the organized church for a season. I was like Moses. For everything that came at me, I went to a secret place to inquire of God. I was so careful not to do anything out of my own understanding. The year continued, and I remained faithful until I hit a plateau about mid-2018. Disbelief was a factor. Journeying alone was also a factor, and I was slowly losing my way. Then it got to the point where I was okay with losing the way. My mind was slipping, and my challenges began.

I started writing this confession on May 15, 2019, because I realized how far I had strayed from my place with the Lord. And I was about tired of it, considering I knew God was not finished with me. I remembered all that God had done for me in 2017, and I knew it was something more to it. So, I began reflecting on how I got to this plateau and what has been keeping me here. I understood that I had reached this point in my life due to a lack of focus. I no longer felt like I belonged to anything. There was no accountability and no support, so I stopped the work. I made this wilderness all about me. I stopped asking God for direction. I remained in such a place because I had become complacent, lazy, and okay with doing nothing. It had made me insensitive to the divine work. I did not trust anybody because, in a sense, we are all out for ourselves. I especially did not trust the church anymore. But with all of this, now I wanted to serve myself in my flesh. I no longer wanted to be kept. Temptation had found a way into my mind, and the more I entertained it, the more I no longer wanted to uphold the standard of righteousness. I just wanted to let go. I would gain hope, but then I would let it go. I did not know how to be consistent anymore, or I did not want to be consistent? I could see the war taking place, but not between God and Satan, yet with the angels and demons.

I took to writing in my journal in May of 2019 because I had to see my confession in black and white. I had to face the shame and guilt in hopes of being able to deal with it. Talking with someone was out of the question. I had lost complete trust in people. This was my only resort. Write it out and look at yourself. I had to look it straight in the eye rather than hide it in my mind, and I was unsure what would happen next, but I did it.

Quoted directly from my journal.

"Okay, so, here it is. The moment is here. The moment I have been waiting for, seeing my confession in black and white. This is my accountability, but it will be difficult to read it again. Here goes nothing.

I have fallen in love with a married man. Oh my gosh, this is ridiculous. I am cringing right now. Or I should say, I have developed feelings for a married man because it is not love. According to 1 Corinthians 13:5, "Love does not demand its own way." Having desires for a married man is my way and not God's way. Now, LET-ME-BE-CLEAR, I have NOT done anything inappropriately with this man by any means. They are just feelings, no actions. However, I am afraid of eventually acting out on my feelings and thoughts. I do not want them to become my actions, as the commonly known quote.

*"Watch your thoughts, they become words,
Watch your words, they become actions,
Watch your actions, they become habits,
Watch your habits, they become your character,
Watch your character, it becomes your destiny" (Tzu, 2022)*

This quote is so powerful. It holds so much depth. I do not want my thoughts to become words of seduction to him and my words to manifest in my actions. The good thing is, I have not boastfully spoken this outwardly to anyone. I have no reason to. Especially to the wrong person, one who would condone such behavior would push me to follow through with my thoughts, but my silence has been my defense."

Once I wrote this out, I was so free within myself. Yes, it was hard at first because it was a poor reflection of me, but facing it gave me so much liberation and power over it. As I mentioned at the beginning of the confession, this was my accountability. I could focus and redirect my mind on God's standards and desires for me and not my own.

I continued to write. I wrote for days. Before I knew it, this confession turned into over thirty pages. God was unveiling so much to me concerning where I was and how I had reached such a dishonorable place. My wilderness season required me to seek God for counsel every day, but at a point, like Israel, I took my eyes off God. I could not see ahead anymore, and I felt like God brought me out of the organized church with no cause. I no longer had the fellowship, the structure, obligations, and responsibilities. Those things had become lifelines to me as Egypt was Israel's lifeline. I could no longer question why Israel struggled to believe God in their time of testing. Years ago, when I started to grow in the word of God, I was studying Israel's journey before their wilderness, in their wilderness, and after their wilderness. I was disturbed by Israel's behavior towards God. God was so merciful to them; He gave them chance after chance, and every time they messed up, as if God did not overlook their previous wrong. I said to myself, "The Israelites were idiots," but my spirit shook after I said it. Then I had an epiphany. I realized I was much like Israel. I was that same idiot. I can no longer question why it was so easy for Israel to choose to give in to their own belief in their time of testing and turn their backs on God after the miraculous signs and wonders He did before them. No longer was I flabbergasted because I was faced with the same pressure and temptation to pursue my results because whatever God was doing was not making any sense.

After all the miracles I witnessed in my wilderness and before my wilderness, I chose to be consumed by my flesh. Jesus said in John 10:28, "And I give them eternal life, and they shall never perish; neither shall anyone snatch them out of My hand." No one or anything diabolical has the authority or power to snatch us out of the hands of Christ. However, we can choose to remove ourselves from His protection and promises. Paul said it best, "We are enticed and lowered away by our flesh" (James 1:14). So, you see, this confession was necessary. It provided healing for my soul and redemption for the grace of God, lost by my sin. This confession brought me out of a dark place.

Deliverance did not come all at once, though. I had to walk the process out every day. Every day I had to resist my thoughts by intensifying my prayer life. I realized the feelings for a married man were simply false illusions. Once I understood this, it became clear that it was not the person I grew fond of but the man. The person represents the character, social relationship, or behavioral patterns. It certainly was not that he was a longtime friend whose views in life were quite different from mine but having the adult conversation was quite refreshing. His character was not something I was attracted to, but simply his nature. He was a man, and the male company was comforting to me, being single for so long. I enjoyed his company, and I fell in love with the moments. It is important to be in tune with the season you are in, always, regardless of whether you are single or married but know when you are vulnerable because entertaining others from the other sex could cause you to compromise. When you compromise, sin gives birth and separates you from God. Knowing this, we must discipline ourselves to think good thoughts and not thoughts to do evil things (Philippians 4:8).

FANTASY ISLAND

In the late eighty's, I remember watching a TV series called *Fantasy Island*. At that time, I do not think I had a clue of what this island represented. It was simply good entertainment. My sisters and I had a nineteen-inch black and white TV in our room, and we anticipated watching each time it came on. This island would allow people from all social classes to come and live out their fantasies for a price. The overseer of the island would give them instructions for the best outcomes. He warned them of not being able to stop fantasies once they began. So they had to choose the fantasy wisely because they had to see the fantasy through till its end, not realizing fantasies could cost them loss and devastation, and they could even be the exception. While I do not remember any specific episodes, I vividly remember the storyline. These fantasies were made to appear real, and they would provide a different outlook on themselves or life overall. Mr. Roarke was the overseer of this island, and Tattoo was his assistant. He ensured a safe outcome for all his guests. A recent version of *Fantasy Island* surfaced in 2020, providing an even more gruesome outcome.

Boredom and idle time can lower anyone into a whirlwind of fantasies. The mind is the playground of evil. If we are not careful, we can find ourselves living our lives in our heads, creating fantasies about how we want life to pan out. The imagination runs wild and is unstoppable because it provides a measure of satisfaction in our heads. These are the secret sins mentioned in the earlier chapter. Oh yes, fantasy island is a secret sin. It is by far the worst way to conduct sin versus sin in plain sight. As mentioned before, man will judge you, but sin in secret is judged by God, which He initiates the consequence, and trust me, it will leave an impression on your life. God will make a permanent decision in your life due to secret sin, all because you chose to be so impressed by your own choices and not ask for an atonement for the sin and turn away. Proverbs 28:13 says, "He who covers his sins will not prosper." Permanent consequences stunt your growth in life and cause missed opportunities. You fail to advance to the next level; you cannot go past go, but instead, you go back so many places until you learn your lesson. Think about the game of Monopoly. In Monopoly, going backward could land you in jail, bondage, or prison. Sin can be described as such; it is bondage, holding you there in contempt and misery.

God does not put us in bondage. Our sins do. Let me make that clear. The other part of Proverbs 28:13 says, "But whoever confesses and forsakes them will have mercy." It is one thing to confess your sin with your mouth, but it is another when you forsake them, meaning no longer practice the sin you have confessed. You must quit the sin, check out of fantasy island, give it up, renounce the habit and abandon them. There must be a turning away, which is challenging for all of us. Sorry is not enough. There must be an honest confrontation of sin. Acknowledge what you did or are still doing, face it, confront it, own it, admit it, and so on, repent, then study the sin no more. It is then we shall obtain mercy, forgiveness, a pardon, compassion, a not guilty verdict, and you are free to go and receive the grace to continue with life. This is God's benevolence for us when we repent.

My dishonorable emotional affair is why I was in confession for about six months. Instead of just acknowledging my sin, I realized I must go a step further and forsake my sin. I took the time to really understand this place in detail, so I did not continue in secret sin.

OVERCOMING TEMPTATION

Jesus was the best earthly teacher on how to overcome temptation. He overthrew Satan after His forty-day forty-night wilderness experience. He teaches us in Matthew 4:1, "Then Jesus was led up by the Spirit into the wilderness to be tempted by the devil." Being called to isolation is nothing new in the world. We see it in both the Old and New Testament, and each time, it was God-ordained. Our wilderness has a purpose: refining, purifying and preparing for the next. Jesus abstained from food and drink for forty days and forty nights. We know that our fleshly body needs daily nutrition to function correctly. Without it, we become weak, and if we are weak, we are vulnerable to anything. Christ, being swaddled in the flesh, was subjected to this weakness. Though He was God in the form of flesh (Philippians 2:6-8), He could feel what we feel. He was subjected to our limitations, and He needed to discipline His flesh. Jesus had such a strength of discipline on Him that could not be broken. Satan tempted Him three times, and each time Jesus overcame Satan's temptation with the Word of God. He did not fight in His own strength because he did not have any. I am sure He was famished in the flesh, but He had something inside of Him far more significant than anything this world could offer. He submitted Himself to the Father, and when Satan came, He resisted him (James 4:7). There is a reward when we overcome temptation. Temptation is what it is, a test. It is a test of loyalty; it reveals what is in you. Jesus' wilderness experience revealed that He was loyal to the call and could stand during times of hardship. Israel's wilderness revealed that they were feeble and were not too sure of their God. My wilderness experience revealed

DISCIPLINE IN THE WILDERNESS

areas in me that needed to die, and with that, during hardship, I tended to seek self-gratification. My loyalty to the call was questionable, and I needed to be more willing even when I did not understand. Once we decide to have self-control over our thoughts and actions, God moves us to the next. In Matthew 4:11, right after Satan attempted to derail Christ, which did not work, the angels came and ministered to Him (giving Him the strength to continue). It was after that Jesus was able to begin His ministry. The reward for overcoming temptation is discovering our true purpose in life.

Chapter Seven

PROGRESS OVER PERFECTION

In 2021, my youngest daughter completed a significant milestone in her life. In May 2021, she graduated from high school and moved to college to study Sports Medicine in the professional healthcare field. She hopes to become an Athletic Trainer or Sports Physical Therapist. Throughout her entire school career, we would always have a conversation about expectations around performance to ensure she would get into a good college. She was not a consistent honor roll student, but she made the honor roll four times in elementary, middle, and high school. By the time she made it to high school, this was the expectation; considering she chose a private high school, I would have to pay tuition all four years. Therefore, if I had to pay, I wanted perfection. I wanted something to brag about with a child performing above and beyond.

Her first year was average. She brought home between 2.5 and 2.8 GPA but never a 3.0 GPA or higher. I never came down hard on her because her average was good also. But on the inside, I would always hope for that 3.0, and she saw the disappointment on my face. I would always encourage her and tell her she could do it. Whenever she did not make the honor roll, I would probe her about needing a tutor. I was willing to do whatever it took to get her on the honor roll. So, now the pressure was on. Each report card was hard for her because she knew that when she came home with it, and once I saw it and realized she did not make it again, here comes another lecture. I do not know what bothered her the most, the lectures, the missed mark, or her questioning her ability to reach that mark.

In sophomore year, she performed at her worst. Her GPA went down to one point the entire year. She had abandoned the expectations to become more focused on her social life. She had an amazing social life, and we both became distracted by it. I firmly believe the pressure of making the honor roll became too much for her, and she left the possibility of reaching it. It was not until the last report card of the year I realized she brought home one point the entire year. Now, I am upset because again, I paid for this one point and, yes, another lecture.

Junior year had to be different. By this time, she was under a great deal of pressure of being removed from the school if the one-point continued. Not by the school, but I would remove her from the highly functioning academic school and place her in another school where I would not have to pay. Because she had fallen so far in the previous year, junior year was even more of a challenge. This time, she set aside her social life and really hit the books. However, she never hit that perfect mark.

At this time, my energy had shifted entirely. Her senior year lecture was not as desperate for honor roll, but I took more of a discovering her ability approach. The drive was no longer honor roll. No, the lecture was vastly different. I asked her what her ideal goal was, the minimum and max. She said, "2.1 to 2.5," I said, "Okay." I had to support it because she is the one doing the work, and she knows her capabilities. I told her, "If you hit your goal or excel it a little bit, you would prove a lot to yourself." Not me, but her. I had to remove myself from her progress eventually. Her first GPA in her senior year was 2.1. She had hit her mark. Uniquely, it boosted her self-esteem. I saw something different in her when she brought her grades home. I saw her confidence increase at that moment, and we celebrated the accomplishment. It is not the honor roll, but it was progress. Once her confidence became extremely high, and she proved to herself that she could hit her marks when they were established with reason, she was able to maintain a 3.0 GPA in her final high school career.

I realized that I was her problem. All those years, I was looking for perfection in the form of the honor roll, and all I had to do was allow her to progress over time. I put so much pressure on her that it may have blocked her ability to retain information, caused her to suffer from test anxiety, and lack confidence in herself.

This is what we do. Sometimes we can want something so bad that all we see is the big picture, that big perfect picture. Once we see it, we gun for it, missing all the steps to gradually move towards the goal. If perfection is the primary pursuit, you can either stand in your own way or stand in someone else's way of progress.

Perfection is an aim to please oneself and even other people. It is common to desire to be perfect at the direst times. When things are not as functional, we require perfection in other parts of our lives. This is self-gratification that we seek to please ourselves. Israel wanted things to be perfect in their wilderness. They wanted the way it once was when they were in Egypt. Though they were in bondage, Egypt provided for them. They found their basic needs being met perfectly for them and their families. When God delivered them from Egypt, all they had to do was obey God, and He would allow them to progress forward within a reasonable amount of time. Still, they only saw that big perfect picture, a home with cattle and food, community, water, etc., so it took them longer to get to the promise as it did my daughter. She could have reached the honor roll mark on her own had I not been so adamant in thinking that honor roll was the only perfect way.

We are perfectly made, but we are not perfect and will never be perfect if we are swaddled in the flesh. The Gospel is perfect, salvation is also perfect, and living your life within the borders of the two allows us to walk in perfect conduct (Matthew 5:48). We can also walk-in perfection when we are willing to examine ourselves and judge only ourselves to see if we are living by faith in Christ (2 Corinthians 13:5).

The laws of Moses were written during times of hardship and used to build the perfect relationship with God, but it turned out the laws were just as imperfect as Israel. The strategy was perfect, and the timing was also perfect, but unfortunately, the further Israel went, the laws just were not working so well. In fact, it stagnated Israel's progress. Israel had a tough time applying all 613 of the laws. I do not believe God intended to bring perfection through the laws, but He wanted cooperation from His chosen people. He only wanted to introduce a plan to Israel to encourage their efforts for perfection in Him. I believe that from the beginning of the creation of time, God knew He would send His Son to die for a perverse generation. Not just Israel, the Jews, but for the non-Jewish people. The Laws of Moses were only for the Israelites, but Jesus was for all humanity which was far more perfect than the laws.

Hebrews 7:11-28 reveals God's plan and ideology of the old priesthood versus the new. Though the writer of the Hebrew letters is unknown, we must know that all scriptures were inspired by God (2 Timothy 3:16).

The writer presents a new covenant that would lead to eternal life. If anyone disobeyed any one of Moses's Laws in the Old Testament, they were immediately put to death. As they tasted death, it prevented them from continuing in the faith or office of a priest. The new covenant changed the order of holiness, which was through Jesus Christ. Jesus was not birthed through the Levitical tribe, nor was He consecrated to serve as a priest, but He was empowered by God to a life that can never be destroyed. Though the laws were not enough, and no one had been found perfect under them, it was still progress. These laws were a sense of forward movement towards God and would bring about personal growth and development.

It does not pay to harp on what religion or doctrine you follow. Religion does not make one perfect, nor does it put us on a path to perfection.

Instead, it can blind us and move us away from having a true relationship with God. The laws were like a religion to the Israelites. They had security through their structure, but they missed the mark every day. Let us not be like the Israelites, holding fast to the covenants made with the forefathers, but let us seek God today for the new in our lives, putting away the old, keeping the covenant of Christ, and creating new covenants daily with Him as we can now strive to perfection without being put to death.

KINGDOM STAKEHOLDERS

The definition of kingdom is "The domain over which the spiritual sovereignty of God or Christ extends, whether in heaven or on earth" (Dictionary.com, 2022). In the same reference, stakeholder means "A person or group that has an investment, share, or interest in something."

God was trying to get Israel to something, as He is also for us. We do not see it right away because of the obstacles in front of us. Once Israel crossed over the Red Sea, they wandered, and they wandered for centuries. Their doubt, disbelief, fear, and disobedience were a precursor of their wandering. They could no longer see the purpose of why they were rescued from bondage. Like Israel, we prejudge what we do not understand. When they faced hardship during their transition, they began to despise their freedom. During COVID-19, everyone went through hardship. We were stuck at home, facing things that were so desperately avoided for days, such as deep cleaning, decluttering, and self-examination. Extroverted people really suffered as they lived for the limelight. Children were stressing out their parents and vice versa. There was depression, financial hardships, lack of supplies, broken marriages, and domestic violence. Social media was flooded with assumptions, panics, and mayhems. The COVID-30 was a revelation. The quarantine ordered by the government mandated everyone to stay home. During this time, binge-watching your favorite series on TV was a thing, and while doing so, you overly indulged in eating and, as a result, excessive weight gain. Unfortunately, we cannot control everything that goes on in life and the world because I am sure we would have been better prepared if we had known this would happen. COVID-19 changed buying and selling as life slowly moved from face-to-face interaction to buying online.

So, why the change and why now? In the days of old, God always revealed to the prophet His coming judgment. Before He released His wrath (Amos 3:7), the prophet would have clear insight on what to tell the people and how to prepare them for what was to come. Obviously, today's world is different from what they were in the ancient days, but I surely believe those who are true prophets saw something coming. Then some inquire of God for instruction in the moment. Though the world has suffered significant losses, God is still on the throne, and He has a greater plan.

Israel's troubling transition eventually moved them into their promised land, where they would always have much more than what they were used to. God was transferring ownership to the Israelites, making them stakeholders of that land, though occupied by other tribes. God was establishing His kingdom amongst Israel. He wanted to get them to a place where they would honor Him daily for all the wonders He did for them while taking care of the land and possessions. In the Book of Joshua, Moses dies. God took his ability to enter the Promised Land when he disobeyed Him in Numbers 20:7-12, striking the rock after God told him to speak to it. We understand Moses struck the rock out of his frustration towards the people. It is like that sometimes, but obeying God is essential. Joshua took them to the Promised Land, where once they arrived, they had to overthrow the inhabitants living there.

Once they fought for their land, God began to divide it among Israel, giving each tribe its own portion. God made them stakeholders of the land, which they could call their own after living under such hardship as slavery. They went from enslaved people to landowners. The minute we are faced with opposition, we should never discount the season because we do not understand, and it is not what we planned, but always look at the big picture and the even bigger person behind the opposition.

COVID-19 was supposed to bring about change to everyone, not just one culture of people, but we all need to get something out of this pandemic. God is kingdom and not community. He wills for no one to perish (2 Peter 3:9), and therefore, unprecedented times must come to alter the minds of the people. But most importantly, what is God trying to get us to? If God is kingdom, being that He extends His spiritual sovereignty to us, and kingdom means domain, a territory governed by Him. It is evident through COVID-19 that His intended purpose is to get people to something. It is a new mindset to change how we see things, a new business or venture. He was offering a stepping out on faith. Look again and ask of Him. For me, He removed my limitations, and 2021 would be the year of the first. In that, He is making me limitless in the way I think. This would be the year I purchased my first home, published my first book, and had my first daughter go to college. I am documenting them as they come. We must believe that God is doing a new thing in the land, and He is calling us to come up a little higher with Him. Our prayers must be "Thy kingdom come; thy will be done on earth as it is in heaven." (Matthew 6:10). Calling on the kingdom of God aligns the mind and will with God, understanding that even in the marketplace, we are not working jobs, but we are positioned to do divine work through our God-given gifts.

SONS/DAUGHTERS OF ZION

Zion is a mountain in Jerusalem, where the temple was built. It was once only a worship center for the Jews, also known as the City of David and the mountain of the Lord in Revelations. This was a place that represented the Kingdom of God. Isaiah referred to it as the Rock of Israel. Romans 9:33 and 1 Peter 2:6 say that in Zion, a stone would cause the people to stumble, and that stone is Jesus Christ. He was rejected by many (His own), but God chose him (1 Peter 2:4), and through this precious Stone (Jesus Christ), non-Jews would no longer be outsiders living in the world (Ephesians 2:19). God's plan was that Jews and Gentiles who believe in His Good News would share the inheritance (Ephesians 3:6). Believers everywhere would become a part of this epic center and His promises.

Even though non-Jews were not God's first chosen, we were engrafted into the promise when we accepted the Lord Jesus Christ as Lord and Savior. We share in the same blessings as being favored by God. "For as many as led by the Spirit of God, these are Sons of God" (Romans 8:14). We do not question His decisions, but we trust Him as our Lord, and with a willing heart, we follow Him. Being a son/daughter of God requires confession with the mouth and heart, and a true son/daughter eagerly desires to hear His voice, allowing Him to lead by His spirit in good and troubling times. As a child would yearn for its parent's voice, it is with our relationship with God. Though Israel was God's first chosen people, they too did wickedness in His sight. They lived a life pleasing themselves while upholding the statutes of the law. It is obvious the law was not enough to keep them in line with the will of God. The laws were written on tablets but not on their hearts, which displeased Him. It was their disobedience that landed them in bondage.

As a son or daughter of the Gospel, it requires great sacrifices, living sacrifices, not dead ones. When I think about the nature of God the Father, as parents, we mirror His standard of parenting (for those who have a child(ren)) when approaching our duties. We expect our children to follow our rules. Whether they are written down on not, there is a curfew on school nights, and they better be home before time. We want the house to look a certain way and expect them to maintain it. We want our child(ren) to do good whether we are looking or not; we hope they would conduct themselves appropriately everywhere they go. And it is all for their good, as we are only trying to get them to something in life. Well, that's God with us; that was God in the wilderness with Israel. We cannot expect our child(ren) to listen to us, and we do not listen to our heavenly Father. It is not enough to be just readers and hearers of the Word but also doers (James 1:22-24). When we become doers of the Word of God (spending time), the relationship with Christ is established in our hearts. As with our child(ren), when we spend time with them and learn to relate to them, it establishes a relationship that when our child(ren) is faced with something hard to talk about, they will have no problem bringing the issue to you. What a privilege to be called a daughter of Zion.

Chapter Eight

RESET

I remember when I purchased my first computer. I worked in corporate America, and we received a subsidy to buy a Dell computer at little cost. When I learned this, I jumped on it immediately. It was a wonderful opportunity to become more familiar with having a computer at home, considering they were becoming more popular during that time. My daughters were in preschool and elementary, so it was also a way to teach them to use the computer appropriately. I purchased the big back desktop and placed a desk in the living room corner. I ordered AOL dial-up internet (times have changed for the better), bought a computer chair, and me and the girls would play on it all night. My oldest daughter used to draft papers all the way up to middle school. She loved playing games that she started downloading from the internet. *Kids Next Door* was her favorite. Not knowing the detriment of the computer being exposed to viruses, I began buying her computer games. Oh, it was next-level technology. Over time, we had downloaded so much on the computer that the computer suddenly started to move slowly. It became very glitchy. Considering I took out the service warranty, I called the Dell warranty center one day while the girls were napping. The representative remoted into my computer to discover that the computer was full of viruses and spyware. At that moment, he educated me on the danger of downloading various software. On top of that, we had no protection on the computer that would alert us if something were not safe. We were vulnerable while having an enjoyable time. I ended up having to reset the entire system to get it to run smoothly again. I spent five hours resetting the computer because of my lack of education about spyware and thinking all those downloads were safe. It took my entire Saturday to clean out my desktop. My girls needed access to a computer at home, and the time was well spent.

All the knowledge my computer retained through downloads had to be emptied. What was there did more harm than good. It could no longer function as it did when I first purchased it. We could not get the best out of it anymore.

Israel's disobedience landed them in captivity for four hundred years. While they were there, their minds became conditioned to their surroundings. But God had greater in mind for them. His intention was not to leave them there forever. He had a set day of their release. He also had a set strategy for how He would set them free and reset them. To reset is to start fresh and continue better than before. Therefore, it brings about a shift around us or in us. After a reset, we should never expect life to be as it once was. What does this say to the time of COVID-19? What is God trying to deliver you from or out of? What is God resetting in your life? What have you been avoiding that really needs your attention? What did you discover about yourself or around you? Did you face it? It is quite possible that God allowed this pestilence to come into the land to get our attention, to move us away from something and to something. Although we do not know what His plans are fully, what we can take from this is He slowed life down to get our attention. We live in a time where people do not want to be saved, and they are not looking for the Savior. We do not want to be saved for real and separated from our sinful nature. The soulish nature of man has fully taken over the conscience of man. God is a jealous God, enough is enough, and here we are.

I went through an extended reset period in my life. I was reset, transitioning from Baptist to non-denominational, then from non-denominational to the wilderness. We unknowingly take that same mindset when we leave something we have practiced for a long time. When I left the Baptist religion, I was no longer in a box, but there were still traits of the old mindset. When I became non-denominational, though I was exposed to a deeper faith and relationship with Christ, those weekly routines and practices were still a major priority. They often came first, even before God. The old traditions had followed me to my new faith. My new faith brought me freedom in discovering Christ, but as time went on and as I look back, I can see the simplicity of religion and the limitation that comes with it. I continued this way for sixteen years.

Resetting is not a terrible thing, but it removes the untuneful, old, non-useful things that no longer work for the cause. To reset is good for the body, soul, and spirit. Though we will suffer loss in times of shifting, it is a season worth embracing. When I reset my computer, I lost so many important files, and my daughter lost school assignments. During COVID-19, I lost friends and loved ones. During Israel's lengthy time in their wilderness, they lost elders during the journey. In 2017, in my resetting time, I lost connections as I transitioned into my wilderness. I tried to resist the reset by holding on to the familiar, but God's will was much stronger, and eventually, those connections were gone. It is essential not to hold on to the old when God is trying to bring us into something new. If we cooperate with the work God is doing on the earth, He will bring us into wide places, and we will be released from restrictions that have kept us from moving freely with the flow of His spirit. These restrictions have resulted from our interaction with other people and our choices. Now is when we can establish ourselves in greater freedom than we have ever known. John 8:32 says, "And you shall know the truth, and the truth shall make you free."

Before my wilderness season, my mindset was practical and routine. I was indoctrinated and fashioned after church obligations, programmed for church as usual. Nothing was more important in my life than my daughters and church. And sometimes, church obligations came before them. Nothing ever interrupted my church routine: Sunday morning service, Tuesday night Bible Study, and Saturday morning prayer. I dare not let anything interfere with these three days out of the week. I was committed to serving in the church, just like my grandmother. I never learned to evangelize effectively, and I remember being afraid to do such a thing. I could not fathom the words to say to win a soul to Christ, so I would invite them to church and pray they received a message of hope. Authority was given to Christ, and He commanded us all to make disciples of all nations (Matthew 28:18-20). Spending time with Christ builds our confidence to testify before one or great multitudes. Not reading the word of God or creating quiet time with the Lord restricts us from moving one with God in the spirit. We become lukewarm and afraid to testify. Sometimes we lack the mindset to ask God to equip us for the greater works outside the church. My wilderness season taught me to prepare for a bigger platform that would look nothing like a pulpit but wide-open places where I can testify of His goodness.

We must be willing to reset, to change the pace when God says it is time. One morning during my workout routine. The Lord spoke these words to me, "Change the Pace." My workout routine has been the same for years. I walk my treadmill for about 30 – 45 minutes three times a week or sometimes five days a week. My routine consisted of walking with ankle weights at a 3.1 speed for thirty minutes, then 6.5 incline at 2.6 speed for five minutes, removing the ankle weights, no incline, and jogging for five minutes, the last five minutes a slowdown then stretching (creation of habit). I worked out this way consistently for three years.

I usually work out at night, but I decided to try the mornings before work this week. I use my phone and Samsung Gear earpieces, and off I go. But one day, as I started my routine, I kept getting interrupted by work obligations and personal calls. My phone kept ringing, or a text would come in. I could have easily ignored it and waited until I was done with my workout, but for some reason, I had the urge to stop and answer, and yes, the calls needed my immediate attention. After about four interruptions and losing time, I continued my workout, but the routine was broken. I walked for about ten minutes within the thirty minutes on the treadmill, and I wanted to get the run in, and I knew I was not going to have enough time to go through the whole routine. At that tenth minute, I heard God say, "Change the Pace." I knew exactly what He was talking about. He wanted to change the routine I had created and been faithful to for three years. When I heard Him, I immediately started my jog, only ten minutes in the routine. The routine I had been so faithful to for years had been interrupted.

When we show ourselves faithful to something, God uses change to evaluate our loyalty to Him. He can use any area in your life to see if you would trust Him and obey, like Abraham's ultimate test of faith with the sacrifice of Isaac (Genesis 22). God did not want this man to kill his own son, the promise. He only wanted to assess and see if Abraham would listen. When life changes drastically or subtly, it behooves us to listen to the still small voice of God as it is only a test to see if we will obey. If God can trust us with the little, He makes us ruler over much more (Luke 16:10).

RECONDITIONING THE MIND

This lesson of a wilderness can be hard if you are not fully in tune with what God is up to. We understand Israel was in Egypt for 430 years. We also understand that they had become fashioned and accustomed to their place of bondage. Their mindset had been completely altered from what they were used to and more on Egypt's way of life. In Exodus 5, it is obvious that the Israelites were enslaved people in Egypt. They were forced to make bricks out of straws that the Egyptian leaders provided. The use of these bricks would build temples. Pharoah ordered them to labor for no wages. He became upset when he encountered Moses with God's command to let Israel go. Pharoah instructed his leaders to withhold supply (straws), preventing them from making more bricks (very spiteful). With less supply, Pharoah still expected them to produce the daily quantity of bricks, and if they did not meet the daily production, they were beaten severely. The Israelites were not brick makers, but they certainly were no strangers to building. They grew even more accustomed to this kind of work, building on their land to building and crafting in bondage. Though they did not pay for their labors, they had shelter, food, and water when needed. This life had become theirs and their children's normal.

God planned to first get them out of Egypt. Once they were set free from their captor, He continued to work miracles to prove to them that He was with them and in control. God wanted to gain their trust through the process. Therefore, after the Red Sea crossing (Exodus 14), in the wilderness, they went. This was only intended to be a seven to eleven-day journey; however, with Israel's mindset, it took them much longer to get to the promise.

Israel lived under confinement for centuries. Their elders had died in bondage, and many were birthed during these challenging times, and now they were free and in the wild with no direction. The only thing they knew was labor, torture, and grief. For anyone coming out of confinement, it is a necessity that instruction or guidance is provided to live a normal life again, not to rehash and hold on to the old normal but to fit in the new normal. Israel needed discipline in building a relationship with God, their Deliverer, the same discipline they had in Egypt building for Pharoah. By the time they reach Mount Sinai, this would be the place where their training of discipline would begin, God's creation of the laws through Moses. These laws were first to remove the old mindset and teach Israel how to live and develop a relationship with the God who delivered them from bondage in this new place they had been placed in. Israel had to learn to trust God. They had to learn to hear His voice and not harden their hearts when they heard it. The laws were established for Israel as part of God's treatment plan for a set time. Israel needed treatment after being captive for so long.

Anytime you are in an environment set to function a certain way, it brings consequences for operating outside that structure. Once you have been removed from such harshness, you must unlearn the behaviors developed through confinement and even be healed from any form of trauma.

The Black American ancestors were released from slavery with no treatment plan offered by their oppressor, and they did not want to be free. They were free and had no means of direction. They were not equipped to function normally in a society that dehumanized them. They struggled to care for themselves and their families. They had no clue what they needed and could not read or discern; they were like lost little children.

God did not enslave Black people, but the evil that paraded the heart of wicked people did. When God brings one into confinements, He is gracious enough to ensure a plan is in place to discipline that life back to His standards. Israel is a prime example.

The Laws of Moses were designed to fashion Israel after God's standards. Israel had to practice these laws so that they would please God with their lives. Under God's counsel, Moses wrote 613 laws that Israel would have to keep in their hearts (see throughout the letters of Moses)—upholding all of them daily. This surely seems a little unreasonable to expect of a people who could barely believe God after witnessing miracles. Still, it was necessary for them because their minds needed to be reconditioned between bondage and their wandering in the wilderness. They had to unlearn so much they had become accustomed to over time.

A plastic surgeon in the 1950s by the name of Maxwell Maltz observed his patients making behavioral changes after surgery in a minimum of twenty-one days. In his book titled, *Psycho-Cybernetics*, he made a distinctive observation of old ideologies leaving and new ones forming in his line of work. Depending on the person, it took a minimum of twenty-one days or more to develop a new concept or undo an old concept. Jesus fasted forty days before He began His ministry in Matthew 4. In verse eleven, after He was tempted by Satan, the scripture says, "The angels came and ministered to Him." It is safe to say the forty days prepared Him to withstand his temper. The angels ministering to Him is significant to the twenty-four angels at the throne of the Father ministering to Him twenty-four seven. Therefore, this can be viewed as Jesus' model of self-discipline when serving God. The angels witnessed Jesus become like human form and suffer the agony we suffer every day in the flesh. They observed Him humble himself and become low like man. Just as they served God on the throne, they also served Jesus throughout His ministry on the earth.

Anytime change approaches our lives, voluntarily or involuntarily, it will take time for one to fully become disciplined with the new. We must be open to new seasons even if it does not look the same as the old. The more the days go by, the closer we are to the final days (Hebrews 10:25).

PUT AWAY THE OLD

"And no one puts new wine into old wineskins; or else the new wine will burst the wineskins and be spilled, and the wineskins will be ruined. But new wine will burst wine must be put into new wineskins, and both are preserved. And no one, having drunk old wine, immediately desires new; for he says, 'The old is better.'" (Luke 5:37-39)

The way you think will determine how you will perceive this section. I encourage every reader to be open-minded and take on an unfamiliar perspective on what we call religion today, the routines we engulf ourselves in, and our religious practices, where it has gotten you in life and your private life. How successful are you in your private devotion with God? How often do you pray to God? Is your faith in God or church tradition/people? Are you growing spiritually? Are you guilty of operating in the old under new seasons?

For centuries leaders have taken portions of the laws of Moses and incorporated them into their daily services. I grew up in the church;

DISCIPLINE IN THE WILDERNESS

therefore, I am aware of all the expectations of church members. As I mentioned before, my mind was still fashioned after church ideology in my wilderness season. I felt convicted for not being in a church on Sunday morning or Bible Study on Tuesday nights. When God called me out of the church, I assumed He was calling me to another church. When I finally yielded to the Lord, I realized He had called me away from the church for a season. He ministered to me on His standard for my life, and it just so happened to look nothing like the church.

One of the most significant false doctrines in the church is tithing. Tithing was one of the 613 laws of Moses (Leviticus 27:30-34) that was used to discipline Israel. Tithing was a tenth of agricultural produce. Each time tithing was required for Israel, there were specific instructions, which can be found in Numbers 18:21,24, Deuteronomy 14:22-27, and Deuteronomy 14:28-29. When Israel possessed their land, God divided the land among all twelve tribes; however, the Levites, being designated as the priest of the land, did not receive any portions of the land. God would build the temple for them, and they would labor in it all their days. God left them responsible for the temple for the atonement of Israel's sins. The Levites did not have crops and supplies to build on, so in Numbers 18, God granted the tithe to be paid to the Levites, the elders in the temple. While they tended to God's business, God tended to their business. All the tithes God mandated Israel to pay went to Aaron and the priest. These tithes were to benefit the collector and aid God's children to trust Him in every way and provide for the poor. They did not harp on tithing and pressure others to give, but each was required to give if they were willing, obedient, and wanted to experience God's blessings.

Tithing today is completely out of hand and far from its original origin that even the poor are pressured to pay tithe. It has come to your home life being cursed if you are not tithing. There is and has been a misuse of the tithe in the church today that God is not pleased with. I learned this in my wilderness. God not only called me away from the church, but He also called me away from the church's practices. It was proven that there is no curse associated with not tithing. How could I tithe if I am not a part of the church? I was so afraid of the curse that I prayed that God would show me where I could send a tenth of my income. He did not, and I was a wreck, but I was also going through unlearning what I had been trained to believe all my life. My first year of walking with the Lord away from the church was one of my best and strongest years ever. In fact, I saw much more growth, favor, promotion, raises, recognition, and joy. As the days went on, I became increasingly relieved of this new journey, and it was easy for me to see and obey God. I also learned to obey even when I could not see. The Laws of Moses were established to restructure the mind of Israel so they would be a service to God, being His first chosen people. Israel did not have the option to obey only the laws that were more applicable to them, but they had to apply all the laws to experience God's blessings. If they broke any of these laws, they were subjected to death. Paul said in 2 Corinthians 3:6, "The letter (law) kills, but the Spirit gives life," and Romans 7:6 says, "But now we have been released from the law… and that we serve in the new way and not the old way the written code." Now, the laws of Moses can be used as principles today. These principles help all believers live a life in Christ, but these laws are not to be placed above God. If one decides to live according to most or all the Laws of Moses, that becomes their personal conviction. Conviction is not to be given by man, but conviction comes through having a personal relationship with the Lord, and He convicts based on willingness and personal vows. We must examine what our faith is in. Meaning, do you trust the tithe, or do you trust God? God will put your faith to the test to see if you will follow Him or rituals. He reveals where our faith lies, and anytime we are not willing to see, He will call for a wilderness-like season, a season of stripping, loss, dryness, fatigue, and unfamiliarity that will draw you closer to seek Him for answers.

The times we live in are perilous; therefore, we must be willing and obedient to put away idolatry, old customs, practices, religions, and rituals, none of which will benefit the believer. God wants to do something new through you.

CHURCH IS NOT ENOUGH

"Making the word of God of no effect through your tradition which you have handed down. And many such things you do" (Mark 7:13). I started serving in the church at a tender age. However, it was because I had to and not because I wanted to. When my parents were still married, they served as an usher and a deacon at a Baptist church along with my mom's sisters and other relatives. In fact, my mother's mom also was an usher at her home church in Memphis, TN, and when we visited, I always took pleasure watching her serve. As a child, I did not fully understand why it was necessary to serve in the church. Because there was never a connection established between God and serving, I grew tired of it over time. At some point, despising it. Once I turned seventeen, that was my time to go in another direction, and I eventually left the church.

My parents were born and raised in Tennessee. My father is from Covington, and my mother is from Memphis. They both migrated to the Midwest at a young age when factory jobs were evolving. We were middle-class citizens making the best we could out of life. My parents married and raised four children together until their divorce when we were young. During their marriage and after, about every year, we would travel as a family to visit the south, mostly my mother's side of the family in Memphis. These were the best times as we would travel in about five to six cars trailing each other while using walkie-talkies; cell phones had not emerged yet, so they improvised to stay connected with each other while on the road.

They were proud of their Baptist background. In fact, this is all they knew and ever wanted to know. Every Sunday, the family would gather at the big house in Memphis, and we would all leave for church together. I remember my grandmother used to transform for church. Her usher uniform was like a super-suit as she prepared to serve at her local church. She would put on her white one-piece dress that buttoned down the middle, with her gold pin on the left of her breast. She had these fancy cat eyeglasses that she would only wear for church on Sunday. She put on her neat gray and black wig and was ready. We would head off to church, and once there, I watched how diligently she served the church. I remember watching her as she watched over the congregation, ready to serve anyone in need. I could tell she was so proud of what she did. It is fair to say it gave her a sense of belonging. She did not have to worry too much while there; it was like a place of escape from something, even a haven for her.

My grandmother was born in the mid-twenties. She never talked about the horrible things she may have witnessed during her days, but we know she saw things and even experienced the hatred sprung from White people. It is also possible that what she saw scared her so bad that it killed her motivation to go beyond the box she was living in. Every time I would look at her, she always had this toughness about her. Her strength seemed unbreakable. But underneath all those layers, she was angry, sad, and afraid. I often wondered if my grandmother ever dreamed or hoped for something. What were her aspirations? She only had a third-grade education. Her mother died when she was only eight years old. She was left to fend for herself and the other children being a child herself. She married my grandfather, her husband until she died in 1996, and my grandfather passed away years later. She was a caregiver for her paraplegic brother, and she maintained the household.

It is evident why the Black church's expression of faith is much more radical and stronger than other races. The oppression Black people faced during slavery was simply cruel. Our ancestors were taken against their wills from their own land to be brought to a country that would degrade them. They were placed in the pit of ships, beaten, sworn at, and died in the pit of these ships or were even thrown overboard, stripping them from their families and desecrating them. They experienced hell on earth, and all they wanted was heaven on earth. From their torture and cruelty came the "Negro Spirituals." Negro Spirituals like "Nobody Knows the Trouble I've Seen," "Steal Away," "Go Down Moses," and "Swing Low, Sweet Chariot." These songs were a plea for help and comfort in their times of disparity. As time has continued, these disparities still exist, only they have shown up differently. Black people today are still the most targeted and sought-out race to destroy. So, like our ancestors, we find our sense of belonging in our churches, singing songs no one will ever understand.

I watched a story about the famous singer Billie Holiday called *The United States vs. Billie Holiday*. The movie took place during the 1940s. She was a successful artist yet struggling with drugs and her past. Ms. Holiday was so tired of the horrible lynching in the black south that she wrote a song from her soul called "Strange Fruit." The strange fruit hanging from trees were the Black bodies put there by White men. This song questioned the poor behavior of people that called themselves Christians. How could such fruit hang from trees with blood dripping into the roots of the trees? It was because of this song that Ms. Holiday became a target. The government feared that it would put ideas in people's heads and cause rioting. Because she was a struggling addict, instead of the system stepping up to help her, they put the narcotics division on her to shut her up. She was relentless, but so was the government.

I thought about my grandmother and other young Black people back then while watching this movie. My grandmother was a teenager during Billie Holiday's career. It is very well possible her young mind saw how this woman who looked just like her was being treated because of the message of her song. The public disparities Black people faced undoubtedly have caused suffering in silence, completely shutting down any aspirations because what happened to Billie Holiday could happen to other Black people during that time. My grandmother may have been scared to dream big or dream at all. If the system can make an example out of Ms. Holiday, this is like a message to other Blacks. If you have a message that would cause others to rise in power, you too will become a target. Therefore, she did not dream of more or different, and home and church became her haven.

I am sure other Blacks and my grandmother did not feel like they belonged in society, so they flocked to their religions for comfort. Going to church every Sunday, Sunday School, Bible Study, paying their tithes, singing in the choirs, serving on auxiliaries,' attending conferences, conventions, and many other church functions provided a belonging. What I have found in all the busyness is that there was no real relationship with Christ. There has never even been an encounter with Him. In other words, there was never a day of salvation in their lives. These religious traditions and practices have been passed down within Black families from generation to generation. I have great sympathy for my ancestors and elders for what they experienced and understand they did what they had to do to get by and, most importantly, to survive. However, because these practices were birth through oppression, they did not discover the full truth of the Gospel of Jesus Christ. There is still more to learn about our Savior. Therefore, religion, doctrines, and church are not enough. There is no power in serving in the church. You will not find deliverance for your soul singing in the choir. The goal and the purposes of these practices should build your character, but you cannot find salvation through them. I cannot say if my grandmother was or was not saved. It is not my place to, but I can say I never saw her pray, exhort us in the Word of God, pray over us (the children) or talk about her faith in God to us. I cannot say she was a prayer warrior or an evangelist, but I can say she was Baptist.

The use of religion and their traditions was to get them closer to God, when in fact, the tradition that comes through religion hinders that connection with God, and we must be careful not to put tradition above God. It is extremely easy for us not to worship traditions more than we worship Him. Tradition is for preservation, harping on the efforts of keeping a lineage pure or preserving a particular character. However, tradition is made to be broken. We find character-building when we trust God (Romans 5:3-5). God broke His tradition when He sent His only Son, Jesus Christ, to present the Law of Grace.

I cannot recall salvation being extended to me when I was under the Baptist church. In fact, I did not know what it meant to be saved because of all the traditions and routines. Every Sunday, we went to church, looked the part, served on auxiliaries, and listened to announcements. The choir sang A & B selections. There was preaching that put Christ back on the cross, and then He got up early Sunday morning. We collected tithes, raised an offering, and then returned to what life was before. After that, there was no more talk about Christ. For those next six days, it was back to carnal living. Eventually, I left the church altogether at the age of seventeen, as it was not enough, and my quest for salvation would begin at that point.

    I gave my life to Lord on November 6, 2001. I was twenty-four years old and eight months pregnant with my second daughter. I had just gotten out of a broken relationship, unknowingly and unplanned. I fell to my knees at home that night in my bathroom and asked Christ to come into my heart. I could not take it anymore. I felt I had made a complete wreck of my life. That day my life changed, but there was still so much I had to learn about being saved; remember, I did not know what salvation really meant. I returned to what was familiar after having my daughter. I went back to the Baptist church I grew up in and returned to familiar activities I did when I was in the world. While I continued to go to church every Sunday, which I was taught, I fell back into a bed of sin with my daughter's father. It was not an official relationship; I had gone back to what I knew because I did not know how to be kept. I did not possess the faith or skill to ward off my flesh. This went on for about two years until I grew frustrated and screamed in the car after leaving church. I could not understand why I was still struggling this way if I went to church every Sunday and paid my tithes faithfully. I even started going to Sunday School, thinking I would find refuge there, but no, the battle was still on every night. My last strategy was to get on an auxiliary. Yes, that is it! Start serving, and that should do the trick. I never made it to that point. I left church one Sunday, and I screamed so loud in my car, crying, asking God, "What is salvation?" I was hitting my dashboard because I was tired of living two different lives, and it was very taxing. My oldest daughter did not know what was going on with me. I had completely lost it. God answers us when we cry out to Him (Psalm 4:1).

Months went by, and I was invited to a non-denominational church on July 3, 2004. This was a worshipping church. It was different from what I was used to. The church size was around two thousand members of all races, and they had an expression of worship that I could not fathom. So, I watched to understand. Once I understood, I realized God was inviting me into a relationship with Him. The sound of worship coming out of the congregation's mouth was so profound that I knew there was angelic company in the building. I was touched that day through worship, and when I went home, I managed to muster up the strength to resist the temptation that came every night. And from that day until now, I have never practiced that way again. It is the tradition of man that makes the Word of God of no effect. God's promises of deliverance could not fully work for me because of the traditional church mentality handed down to me. These traditions clouded my mind and stagnated the hand of God. Once my mind was changed and set on the things of God, I was reading more of the word throughout the week, I was praying more, and I no longer waited for Sunday to partake in godly things; it had become my lifestyle. Then I realized that God had given me the ability to change tradition and change the way I pursued Him.

Christ was not religious. He was not Catholic, Presbyterian, AME, Church of God in Christ, Baptist, Jehovah's Witness, etc. These doctrines are flawed, missing one thing and adding other things to it to fit the people. However, God will not adjust righteous garments to fit a people. He is not our personal tailor, but He adjusts us to fit His righteous garments. He is our potter.

The organized church is not obsolete, and it is not being replaced with another alternative. However, I believe that what we are used to in the church has had little to no effect on most believers. We must understand there is the church and the organized church, and we must be mindful of the distinctive difference between the two. The church consists of a person. It is the character of God in that person who we carry in our hearts daily. We are made by the hands of God (Hebrews 8:2), and He is the Bishop/

Overseer of our souls. We are the church; we make up lacks and bridge gaps. We are the holy temple of God. The organized church, on the other hand, is established by man. In their own strength and knowledge, man lays a foundation where like-minded believers come to fellowship with one another in a building, and man is the overseer of the organized church. It still has its place and significance in the life of the believer, but every born-again believer carries the responsibility to share God's love with the lost, the troubled, and bound in the hope that they find deliverance in Christ. The organized church must be okay with coming outside of the four walls of the church. The assemblies of God are intended to come together to draw more strength and wisdom to continue. We encourage one another to do better in Christ, not just in church on Sunday or at weekday prayer, but every day of our lives.

A wilderness season will take you places other people will not understand. God will show you things that others will not believe. Because of tradition, they will deny your season because it will go against their tradition, but God calls for us to serve Him through love and obedience. We follow God even if where He is leading us does not make sense to us or others. I received backlashes when God called me away from the church in 2017. I heard Hebrews 10:25 (read it) recited to me so many times. This scripture justified me having to be in church, and because I was not, I was put in a place of disobedience. It is a complete difference when you serve God versus serving the church. When serving God, He can interrupt the place you are in at any moment to send you to your next.

Whether it makes sense to you or anybody else, He will do it anyhow. I do not believe that I am to never return to the church, but I believe it will be different from the last seasons when I return. We must be careful not to be more loyal to church tradition than God. When He leads us on an unfamiliar path, no one else can guide us but Him, and we go with no reservation. These journeys will assess your loyalty to Him and expose what is really in your heart. You must be willing to go, even if others do not agree. Go anyhow!

Chapter Nine

PRAYING & FASTING ARE ESSENTIAL TO A WILDERNESS

When the pandemic started in March of 2020, there was more talk of essential items, so many worldwide rushed to stores to overstock their homes with food, water, tissue, and disinfectant spray. The virus caused a shortage in supplies all over the world. Countries where these supplies would come from completely stopped production to prevent the spread of the virus. Businesses were distinguished from essential to non-essential, and if identified as non-essential, they were forced to close their doors, suffering a significant loss of income. I could not understand how tissue became so much more essential than food during all the hardship. People had found comfort or a newfound faith in tissue. There was a widespread panic that all people could think of was bathroom sanitation. I, for one, buy tissue in bulk which I only purchase twice a year. It just so happened that I was due for another bulk during this time, and what do you know, the tissue aisles were empty, everywhere! Oh, the rage I felt looking at the brick walls at Sam's Club where tissue once sat in front. I was livid! For weeks, I went from store to store, hoping a shipment would have come in, and to no surprise, it had not. I blamed the media for this nonsense. People create narratives that cause uproars, paradigm shifts, and panics through the media. And they did, the narrative of tissue being essential like more than ever; therefore, get all you can. Never mind your neighbor, but every man for himself. I did not panic as I was running low because I knew God was not working through the tissue and that He would provide before I ran out, and He did.

We found ourselves in a place like Israel's wilderness, having to trust God in the unknown, and He has left us up to ourselves; therefore, we created something to trust in. We created idols and found other means of comfort. Israel built the golden calf out of what they had lying around. They used forms of materials to build their god because Moses took too long to come back to them, and they assumed God did something to him. Instead of praying and having patience, they reverted to their ways.

Social media was another crucial factor for answers, from news to narrative and trends to cancel cultures. These things brought a sense of comfort to mind. It kept people from losing it during this downtime. We become most creative when there is nothing else to do, so creative that we make idols. It is easy to do nothing with our spiritual gifts than to keep strengthening them by relying on the source who provided them to us.

In 1 Corinthians 10, Paul warned us of the lessons of Israel's idolatry. They were guided by a supernatural cloud and on dry ground through the waters. They all followed Moses and adhered to his commands, yet God was not pleased with them. Israel lost 23,000 of its relatives because of their actions in the wilderness. The common response God was looking for from them was faith through prayer, as He requires from us in times of crisis.

Prayer is and will always be essential to the life of the believer. Without prayer and the Word of God, we become cold and callous to the will of God. Through prayer, God reveals His secrets to us; it is another channel of communication. The Word of God instructs us to pray without ceasing. If we belong to Christ, we understand this is God's will for the believer (1 Thessalonians 5:16-17).

Prayer produces results. Our spiritual gifts are birthed and revealed through prayer. Revelation comes through prayer. Prayer is simply having a conversation with God. It comes easy when there has been a relationship established with Him. One of the most important keys to a healthy relationship is communication. It is the law of giving and taking, listening, and talking. It is a form of reciprocity, an even exchange. A relationship with no communication is subject to failure. The foundation will always be questionable and feeble. When we pray, we make petitions and wait for the responses. If the line of communication is broken between you and God, it can ultimately lead to low morale. Lack of communication can create a mishandling in life, distrust of those God uses around you, missed opportunities, misunderstanding, misinformation, conflict, and defeat. Prayer prevents all these unfortunate mishaps. Has God revealed your spiritual gifts? If so, are you walking in them? If you are walking in them, you need a prayer life to know how to function in them fully. What do you do when you know God is speaking or summons you? Do you obey? Or do you continue as you were?

I mentor teen boys and girls with the work I do daily. I was spending time with one of my mentees in the community. Her name is Marie. Marie had been diligent for a year with saving money to buy a car once she obtained her license. Over time, Marie would share with me premonitions she would have throughout her day. She was afraid and did not know what to do. They were so evident; she could not ignore them. She heard of God but did not know Him, so these premonitions awakened her interest in knowing more of Him. On this day, Marie and I were at a dealership waiting for her sales rep to close the deal on the car she picked out. She was sharing her night with me, and in her conversation, she said, "I was up praying," brushing past it so I could sense her discomfort with saying such words. Being the oldest, it is easy to talk more because I have been around longer, and one can assume they know more. Not so, we do not know what one is trying to say and where they are going in a conversation, so it is always good to listen to understand rather than listening to respond. I build an open and honest relationship with young people, free from any judgment, hoping they can come to me and share their deepest secrets and not be mishandled. She said, "Ms. Sherie, I was watching a movie last night, and at the end, the actor said, "Maybe this is a sign that God wants me to stop smoking weed." She had this same thought, and here it is in this movie. She immediately said, "I don't know, maybe it wasn't God. I'll ask Him again." All I could say was, "Wait, what?" I had to be incredibly careful with my response because she was not ready to hear what I was about to say. I first recognized that there was a lack of relationship with God. Because when you love someone, and they speak, you value what they say. Without doubt or second-guessing, it is simply yes or okay. Yes, Marie smokes marijuana occasionally. She uses it to function better throughout her day. She believes she functions better under the influence of marijuana versus being sober, not knowing or seeing that she has made marijuana an idol, her god, and she chooses to depend on. If God is speaking to her, and when He speaks to us, he will meet us where we are and build from there. It is up to us to yield to His command and not harden our hearts.

God speaks through His creation. He is the most creative being ever to exist, and yes, He would speak through a movie, commercial, or book. Without a relationship with God or openness to begin one, you can easily miss Him speaking.

Relationships that are unsure are filled with doubt, disgruntlement, discontentment, discord, jealousy, competition, and false realities. Well, Marie had doubts. The message was noticeably clear to her, but there were no depths in the message without the relational component. I talked to her about becoming a believer in Christ. The standard of soberness is vital to the call. 1 Peter 5:8 tells us to be sober and vigilant. Why? Because we have this enemy walking around like a lion, but he is not. In that retrospect, someone who portrays themselves as a lion can come off very vicious (seemingly), and we think we are defeated. However, when we are always sober, we can see beyond Satan's delusion and overcome in seasons.

Prayer is our point of contact with heaven. When we fast, our voices are heard in high places, intimidating anything in the second heaven and moving things in the third heaven. Without prayer, it is hard for one to have a stable relationship with the Father in heaven. Our spiritual gifts will not develop, and we cannot get to God's will in times of crisis because there will be more wilderness experiences. Make prayer essential so that God will reveal His true purpose in the hardship and what is to come.

FIRST RESPONDERS

I accepted the calling of an intercessor ten years ago. As I look back over the preparation and the office, this gift parallels a medical first responder. An intercessor has a unique ability to pray in confidence and authority, standing in the gap to disrupt forces of darkness on another's behalf. Intercessors are very influential people in their surroundings. They are not limited to church walls. People cannot see or believe past the organized church they attend. Intercessors not only pray for their assigned churches they also spiritually cover the entire body of Christ. They not only pray for the cities where they reside, but they pray for nations at a time. Their intentions are to invite the presence of God to favor, protect and provide for others. One who is called to such office must always be ready to yield to the Spirits leading to aid someone who cannot pray themselves. A true intercessor will never go at a task on their own without seeking the counsel of God. When the tides change, we pray, listen, and wait.

We are living in the end of times, and God is revealing to those willing to rise above the stagnation of church tradition and self-doubt and getting us to a place, seeking Him for the greater works beyond the four walls of a building. In critical times the believer's first response to any crisis or unexpected change in life should be prayer. We do not revert to man, gossip, social media, idols, self-pleasures, sorority/fraternities, but prayer. God should be our only resort and not our last resort. Through prayer, He extends answers as we wait patiently. What He reveals belongs to us and our children (Deuteronomy 29:29), meaning we must act on what is revealed. Anyone believed to be called to intercession should expect to operate as a first responder.

Fire Lt. Jared Triplett of Milwaukee, Wisconsin, has been a firefighter for sixteen years. He made a noble decision to become a first responder in the 10th grade when 9/11 happened in New York. During this time, firefighters were more in the public's eye and considering he was born on September 11th, this tragic day would open his heart to join a team of emergency responders. I sat down with Lt. Jared to discuss his role, demands, and sacrifices as a first responder. Lt. Jared is a boots-on-the-ground type of person. Prior to becoming a first responder, he was a lifeguard who earned his medical license. He received extensive training on how to manage life-threatening emergencies.

Lt. Jared began reaching out to his network while still in high school to learn more about becoming a firefighter. Eventually, he was able to start a four-month cadet program in his senior year. He had to undergo rigorous training, and the four-month cadet program would prepare him for the 18-week academy training. He had to excessively run, climb ladders, learn the usage of a fire hose, wear the gear to know what it feels like, and know the limitations, understanding the gear only protects them. He was eighteen when he trained, and he learned that his training was not only physical but also mental.

First Responders are trained to respond to two calls in their stations, one being the Medical Sound, the Emergency Medical Technician (EMT) alert, and two the Ultimate Level of Consequences. This is the final call for a situation, and the firefighters are dispatched. They are trained to know their call by sound and respond by stopping whatever they are doing to adhere to the call. Firefighters do more than just run into burning buildings; they too have an EMT License in which they aid in helping with any medical emergency. They are trained to show up and handle whatever is presented to them.

Lt. Jared talked about the importance of knowing your strengths and weaknesses as a first responder. Lt. Jared's strengths are swift and spontaneous thinking. He remains calm in a situation. He is always the leader and influential one amongst his peers. On the other side, he knows he has weaknesses that he should also be mindful of when on the job: being somewhat of an empath, overly caring in that sometimes he does something nice for someone that his job does not require him to do. Therefore, he works on not being overly consumed by outcomes.

One of the most prominent duties of his job is his sacrifice. He is in the line of fire with a strenuous work schedule, working 48 hours straight, sacrificing time away from his wife and 18-month-old son amid a pandemic. He risks being exposed to the virus each time he goes to work, but that does not stop him from pushing the envelope. He faced a significant challenge: getting a call of four children trapped in a burning building. As he prepared his team to stop at nothing to get those kids to safety, he was determined to move anything that stood in his way of getting to those children. The last thing he wanted to feel was that he had lost those four children, but by the time he and his crew arrived at the scene, the children were out of the building and safe. It was a huge relief. The ultimate feeling for a firefighter is to rescue someone; that is what they are trained to do.

The heroic work Lt. Jared does every day is how he focuses and keeps mentally organized because he remains true to what he does. He keeps his mind sharp through training using job materials, other fellow firefighters' YouTube, policy changes, and other ways to sharpen his skills. He stays studied up. The more training, the more prepared you are for any situation, whether medical or fire. He not only keeps himself sharp, but he strategically trains his crew in distinct functions outside of what they are used to in case one man is down, another one can fill in. I can relate to another one of Lt. Jared's methods of focus, listening to the recording after the emergency. He listens to hear what he could do better. At the start of my wilderness season, I did self-exhortations and prayer audios to keep focus, and I, too, listened back to critique myself.

My final question for Lt. Jared was, what does it take to be a firefighter? He stated, "It takes heart and a willingness to sacrifice." It is obvious the job is not easy as he recalled others in the past had taken this job not knowing there were deal-breakers like blood or vomit. They never reached the level of maturity and growth that allows you to work under any condition. Part of the willingness is to feel and not feel, to find a balance to leading a stress-free life while working a job that could lead to stress. Lt. Jared has this Lion King, Hakuna Matata (worry-free) type demeanor. After the most tragic call, he and his crew can easily return to their station, cook a meal, and sit down and have a rational conversation. It is no doubt firefighters manage stress quite differently from the average person. They have learned to avoid compassion fatigue while connecting with their duties but to disconnect from the outcomes of the duties. Being overly zealous with compassion can be draining and a disservice to yourself and others.

If every intercessor had the mindset as Lt. Jared does when on the job, there is nothing that God would not do or reveal to us in times of crisis that would make us ready in and out of season (2 Timothy 4:2).

FASTING THAT PLEASES GOD

When we fast, we are willing to deny ourselves anything that satisfies the flesh. It exemplifies we are dedicated and devoted to the service and worship of God. In the scriptures, we find that fasting was the perfect form to discipline one to fulfill the call of God. Dr. Tony Evans is one of my favorite vessels of God. He did a mini-sermon on social media in 2020 on Isaiah 58. I studied Isaiah 58 in 2017 at the start of my wilderness season. God revealed so much through this passage. Then in 2020, Dr. Tony Evans had the same message in mind. He prolifically provided benefactors and postures of fasting (Evans, 2018).

- *"Fasting is giving up a craving of the physical to gain assistance from the spiritual.*
- *Heaven comes down and intervenes in our circumstances. Fasting says, "God, I want you in my circumstance."*
- *Fasting improves the lives of others.*
- *God joins me when I call out to Him on behalf of someone else.*
- *Giving up the physical for the spiritual is fuel from heaven that benefits the earth.*
- *We become conduits for God, meaning a channel, passage, or fountain, while being like a cul-de-sac closed at one end, any situation in which further progress is impossible."*

Fasting is not a selfish act. It is selfless. We fast for answers for others and for things to change around. We humble ourselves and allow God to work through us in the situation so that we may see His outcome and not our own. We become a stream for the Spirit of God to flow through us. Fasting makes one increasingly available to the Holy Spirit, and it becomes easier to say "yes" to the most challenging assignments.

In Isaiah 58, God sends Isaiah, the prophet, to rebuke Judah's actions. Judah was once a nation that was righteous before God, but along the way, they too experienced a veering and began to serve God and their idols. While serving their idols, they continued to seek God. Because of these behaviors, Judah's fasting had become ineffective. God sent Isaiah to expose Judah to their evil ways hoping they would turn their hearts back to God. Judah was fasting for all the wrong reasons. They thought they could mix their own ways with God's ways and still get the same results as a righteous man. The prophet revealed to them their hearts in verses 3 & 4, "Why have we fasted, they say, and You have not seen? Why have we afflicted our souls, and You take no notice? In fact, in the day of your fast you find pleasure, and exploit all your laborers. Indeed, you fast for strife and debate and to strike with the fist of wickedness." Judah certainly believed in the power of fasting and how God responds to it, but they failed to posture themselves appropriately for God to move on their behalf. God knows the heart of man, he knows their reasoning for everything, and if the heart is not pure, it will stunt the move of God. Isaiah revealed a treasure to Judah and believers everywhere in the second part of verse four, "You will not fast as you do this day, to make your voice heard in high." When we pray for others, we should want to be ensured our voices are heard in heaven. If there is ever a time you do not feel your voice is heard in heaven, here is the solution to the problem. Isaiah tells Judah that the intention to please God when approaching Him through fasting is the desire to be heard in heaven, not for man to hear you or take you seriously, but for God to hear you and take you seriously. It is far better to allow God to lead you into a fast. He will give you clear directives on what to do and for whom to do it. In July 2019, I was coming out of the season of temptation and still needed to overthrow the fantasy island in my head. I thought I had messed up so bad that I was unredeemable, but there is never a place where God cannot reach His people. As temptation persisted around me daily, on July 1, 2019, the Spirit led me into a seven-day complete fast. A complete fast only consisting of water, which is it, nothing else. I had to do it because it was hard to keep my flesh quiet. During that time, I was aiding other believers with strengthening their prayer life, so I was needed in the kingdom. I could not give thought to the fast because God did it for me. There was no time to waste. By day three, my body ached, my bones were hurting, and I felt weak, but I remained vigilant in praying (where I gained strength). Every day the Lord revealed someone to intercede for. By day six, I felt like death, my ears were ringing off and on, and my physical strength had entirely left my body. My job requires me to serve the community, and I did not take one day off. This fast was necessary.

The pain and grief we carry in our bodies during fasting are what pleases God. In verse five, Isaiah asked, "A Day for a man to afflict his soul? Is it to bow down his head like a bulrush (a bent-over plant)? And an acceptable day of the Lord?" The affliction during fasting is a preparation for the task. An available vessel will carry the grief and pain of others at times, and we will extend them to heaven. This fast was to take my mind off my flesh, i.e., what I eat, what I wear, how to look, and destroy fantasy island. I had obtained a new form of freedom, and every day I had to maintain that freedom the Lord granted me and no longer use my freedom to satisfy my flesh. Fasting is a beautiful process when we go through it properly.

Jesus fasted for forty days and forty nights and was able to resist Satan in His time of weakness (Matthew 4). The rewards are far greater than we can imagine when we fast to please God and not ourselves. It is imperative that we do not fast for carnal reasons, fasting to lose weight to fit in a pair of jeans, or fasting to be seen as more superior than others. Then others fast to obtain wisdom but only boast about it as though they have obtained it independently. These kinds of fasting are not what pleases God. When we fixate our minds on fasting for carnal results, our focus is off during the fast. Extraordinarily little time is offered to God, and we go on with our day-to-day obligations. Then it all just becomes a routine with power in it. There are people who fast for medical purposes or as a health precaution. This is called intermediate fasting. While this is not spiritual fasting, it is to improve the quality of life. There is a reward of good health and preservation of life.

In the Old Testament, Daniel's fast pleased God. So much so that he evolved during the time he and his people were in captivity. The favor of God allowed him to excel and progress during times of testing. Jeremiah was the prophet who prophesied Judah's captivity (read Jeremiah 25:1-11). God had to punish Judah because they had played the harlot even after He sent messenger after messenger to warn them and plead with them to turn back to Him. Judah, however, did not listen. God had had enough of their evil doings, and He caused the Babylonians to take captive of them. They would serve under a wicked king for seventy years. That is a long wilderness, but Daniel, a devoted man of God, excelled in receiving promotion and favor from the king. We excel in God and life when we obey and purpose in our hearts to please God. Daniel did just that. He purposed in his own heart and to God that he would not partake in the king's delicacies. He was in captivity, but he would not become subject to the ways of the king's servants.

In Daniel 1:12-14, Daniel and his three brothers were willingly evaluated to prove to the king that they did not need to eat their foods and that they would find strength with their own modest diet. Daniel petitioned that he and his brothers would eat only vegetables and drink water for ten days. How often while fasting are we placed in an environment with a table spread with pleasant foods? We know we are about to face a table of temptation, so before we lay eyes on it, we start talking to ourselves and encouraging ourselves about what we are not going to do. We try so hard not to fall, and we end up giving in and falling. Once we see that table, we begin reasoning with, "Well, it's just one bite!" We will even abandon the entire fast and never return to it. I have been there! Daniel did not compromise; they were in the presence of so many pleasant foods, but all he could think of was his commitment. At the end of the ten days, Daniel proved that his lifestyle was far more effective in providing strength than the king's food. He and his friend were in better shape and strength than the king's servants (verse 15). As a reward, God gave them knowledge, skill in all literature, and wisdom, and he gave Daniel the gift of understanding dreams and visions, and none were found in the camp like Daniel and his friends. God will set us in places of favor when the commitment is not compromised. Every believer should have a personal fasting lifestyle outside or corporate (organized) fasting. The time spent is well worth it as it improves your health and appearance, makes you more available, and increases wisdom.

Finding peace in our hearts to make a full commitment to pleasing God when fasting is vital. There is mercy for the believers who do not give their lives fully to Christ through salvation. One who refuses to do so could only mean they are not ready to let go of satisfying their flesh, or their lack of commitment derives from a place of fear of falling and not wanting to upset God. Still, His mercy endures forever and to all generations (Psalm 100:5), which means there is a chance you will fall; just get back up.

DEEP AFFECTIONS

"Set your affection on things above, not on things on the earth" (Colossians. 3:2). The best way to survive during a transition is to make sure your desires coincide with God's will. Having a greater desire to see the will of God instead of trying to control the outcome will advance the believer during the transition. You will find out how you love God when a season of change comes upon you. Change can be a challenge when you are used to being in control. But when the affection or feelings are towards God and His plans, nothing stands in the way of progress. Change is not intended to deprive us of courage, but often it is God removing the limits we have operated under for measures of time. A transition will reset our realities so that what we thought was important was not important at all. Every believer should avoid becoming overly emotional or overwhelmed to the point that they become discombobulated, lose confidence, or experience feelings of abandonment, despair, and dissatisfaction. These emotions can cause you to dismiss the season because of a lack of understanding. Considering this, we tend to move away from what we do not understand and often pursue to create another reality just to feel gratified or in control.

The test is to determine whether you can remain fully committed to God our Father during a transition without having a clear picture of what He is doing. Will you still be able to stand on His promises? This poses the question in Amos 3:3, "Can two walk together, unless they are agreed?" Amos, the prophet, proposed this question to Israel along with other questions. Israel had become pompous, being God's first chosen people. They did not understand that God chose them because He wanted to and not because they had special privileges or power. God simply wanted to use them to draw others to Him, that was their God-given duty, but Israel had no longing after the things of God. In fact, they intertwined their idols with the laws of Moses. They had differences in what they wanted to value, and they refused to agree with God, which caused judgment to fall on them. Israel did not advance well in its transition, and that was no one else's fault but their own. It would be difficult to walk with God and not agree, but having a love for Him and all His wonders would cause one to align and agree. When Paul was in prison, he heard about the church in Colosse. They mixed other philosophies with Christian truth, one of which was having special knowledge, denying Christ as Lord and Savior. He exhorted them in Christ's deity, He was God in the flesh, and He died on the cross for our sins. He reminded them of the teachings of the world and that they are of no effect and cannot be compared to God's truths. Therefore, the believer's mind should be occupied with heaven because our eternal destiny has been assured. We should not be found named among worldly lust and sexual impurities. There must be a lesser longing for earthly possessions and a greater longing for our eternal home.

Chapter Ten

THE RED SEA

Israel's crossing of the Red Sea was a huge milestone in their journey. There was so much going on leading up to this part of their journey, as it was only the beginning of their worries. In Egypt, before the Red Sea crossing, they had to endure all ten of the plagues God had inflicted on Pharaoh's land. Though they were there during these devastations, they were not the target. We have seen devastation in the world around us, but not at the magnitude of what Israel had to endure, although cases can be compared to today's time. In Exodus chapters 7–12:

1. The water turned to blood, which left no clean drinking water like when cryptosporidium, lead poison, caused the Flint Michigan catastrophe and other occurrences when the waters were contaminated.
2. An invasion of frogs - a pestilent-like threat because frogs carry bacteria on their skin.
3. An invasion of lice - this is a human infestation that carries uncommon bacteria.

4. Flies, like the killer hornets in 2020.
5. Livestock pestilence - this plague is parallel to COVID-19, causing a limit on supplies throughout the land.
6. Boils are another human infestation.
7. Hailstorms - there are storms throughout our land every season. Storms have risen in places you would not expect.
8. An invasion of locusts - this plague is most common in Africa. Locusts eat at the crops and animals; this limits supply and brings about famine and hunger.
9. Darkness flooded the land, impeding vision and sight. This was to stop the day-to-day.
10. And lastly, the killing of the firstborn child. It seems harsh that God would allow an innocent child to be killed, but it was much deeper than that. He stagnated the bloodline so the evil works in the lineage would not continue. He was protecting the future.

These plagues are overwhelming to take in all at once. Using the New Life Application Bible, the time span of the plagues was about forty days. After the last plague, it was time for them to make their exodus out of Egypt. Everyone had a part in this transition. Moses and Aaron's part was to hear the instructions of the Lord, and Israel was to trust them by conducting the instruction. God had shown them Himself through the plagues, which He allowed Moses to pronounce. Israel had seen the miracles of God; from that and the task at hand, I am sure fear and panic settled in, but they carried out God's plan with precision, got up, packed as much as they could with little preparation, and fled. Every transition requires immediate action, we should not (but we do) sit and ponder on how to do it and when is a suitable time to do it, but when God gives you His plumbline for life, you had better move quickly. There is always a light at the end of the tunnel.

Israel's light was they were no longer bound. However, they had obtained their freedom papers, not knowing what they would face on the journey. During their transition, God took the time to give them His compass of life. They received instructions and standards on how to remember and mark the day He delivered them. God never stopped leading them because He knew the path they would take, and they could not continue without Him. In Exodus 14, they reached the Red Sea. There was no boat or canoe in sight to journey out of the land and away from their adversary. What stood in front of them was the impossible. We are talking about around six hundred thousand men, women, and children with their possessions facing a large body of water. At this point of the journey, we would give up and say, "This is much too difficult. I'm not equipped for this. This is too big. I can't do it." And then we turn back. Our false perception of the task at hand causes us to abort the mission. It is our God-given duty to believe God to do the impossible, and we leave it to Him to do the impossible. The Red Sea was their final transition into safety, provision, and prosperity. They were leaving something and going to something. If the Israelites had not left, their history would be vastly different today. We rewrite the plan of God when we allow fear to grip us into not pursuing the outcome.

Think about a time in your life when you were presented with something larger than life. You had never seen such a thing, and you did not have the answers. And sometimes, whatever it is is so large that fear grips you so tight, and you cannot even believe God for its manifestation. We have all been there. Drafting this book was a challenge. I suffered from the fear of failure and the fear of success. This is called a cliffhanging. I was dangling between two decisions. One, going back to what I know and not taking on such a challenge and avoiding failure, or two, I press forward with authoring the book, and it succeeds and pushes me out of my comfort zone. It would require more out of me. So, I had to choose.

A Red Sea experience can come in other ways. Either way, we can look at it as something, someone, or an event in our life that is standing in the way, preventing us from moving forward. We could be our own Red Sea. Sin could be a Red Sea. An unhealthy relationship, a job, and family members can be Red Seas. We consider what it took for God to move miraculously for Israel at the point of their Red Sea. It took intense prayer for me to overcome the fear of authoring this book. The night I recognized something was wrong, I fell to my knees in prayer, and when I was done, I heard the Spirit say, "Red Sea." At that point, I knew God had parted the sea of fear that I would be able to cross over to the other side of it.

Moses was not the best leader, but he was the best leader for this job because his courage and obedience would lead thousands of people to their freedom. Out of Moses' obedience, God parts this large body of water, causing the walls to form into walls that all six hundred thousand of the Israelites could cross over into another purpose of their journey. They have found their freedom. Think about who is bound around you and you being their freedom rider. We all have a form of leadership in us, and we all lead something or someone around us. It is so vital in seasons of transition that we remain steadfast in our footing as leaders to always obey God, even if what He is asking of you, you cannot fathom it. All we do is obey and believe God for the impossible, and it is His job to do the impossible. In every wilderness, keep the mindset to transition out of it. Avoid becoming comfortable with limitations and old seasons. Thrive frequently on your Christian journey in God.

THE POINT OF NO RETURN

Transitioning into a new normal requires a willingness to leave something behind. We all struggle with leaving what we are comfortable with and are apprehensive about embracing the unknown. Tradition is sometimes to be remembered but often not repeated, for the old can't function in the new. In the synoptic gospels, Jesus makes mention of a parable regarding using the old in the new and how it can be detrimental to the vessels. In Luke 5:33-39, He was answering a question about fasting. The people asked why His disciples were not fasting as much as John the Baptist's disciples and the Pharisees' disciples. Jesus' disciples ate as they walked with Him, and the people could not understand why they were not as dedicated as other disciples. Jesus coming to the earth paints a clear picture of the tides changing, the reformer being amongst them, and the refusal to comprehend it. The disciples' eyes had been opened to seeing the new, and therefore, they began to walk differently. They no longer walked under the laws of Moses. With this newfound knowledge, they knew they did not need to fast as their Beholder was amongst them. Jesus began to talk in parables so that the people would understand, comparing Himself to a new cloth and traditions an old garment. He was the new wine, and the laws were the old wineskins. He warned them that the attempt to use new wine in old wineskins would cause the wineskins to burst and spill the new wine, leaving them both in complete ruins.

This is quite parallel to the times we live in now. There has been a gap between two generations, the new and the old, for the past decade. The older Christians' way is religion, consisting of going to church, church hats, suits (looking the part), paying your tithes, and joining auxiliaries. Still, there is no sign of salvation or relationship with Christ. The old way seemed more self-gratifying than anything else. However, as the generations grew, there was a greater desire for Christianity. The younger generation wanted to know the authentic way to Christ. They did not buy into the old way of Christianity through the church, but there was a greater yearning, i.e., what it meant to be saved, and how even to become saved. Because of the different views, this caused a great divide in churches, and the young people left the church. They left to serve the world as it had more to offer, and then others left to find the way to Christ. You can see the ruins this has brought to the body of Christ. According to the Pew Research Center, Christianity is declining in the United States while non-Christian faiths are growing rapidly (Pew Research Center, 2019). Believers must remain prayerful so that when the seasons change and the error changes, we are not going with every wind of doctrine (Ephesians 4:14-15), but we are aligned with God in the times.

When Christ died on the cross for our sins in the gospels, He left something behind. His sacrifice is a shadow of what it means to transition from something old to the new. He could no longer occupy the body he once lived in on the earth. When He ascended, He reached the point of no return. There was no going back to that old, rugged body that had been beaten and tortured for days on end, but He ascended that He was seated at the right hand of God (Mark 16:19).

Salvation is accepting Christ in our hearts and leaving the old man behind. There must be a refusal to return to the old natures that once had us blind and a slave to sin. There is no going back after death, and all generations must possess a form of discipline to this fact that we do not find ourselves comfortable with rehearsing something God has not approved of on this new journey with Him. In 2 Corinthians 5:17, Paul referenced salvation, "This means that anyone who belongs to Christ has become a new person. The old life is gone; a new life has begun." Jesus received a new life at the Father's right hand; therefore, we should expect to experience an inevitable change when we become His followers. If you are walking with God and there has not been an evident change in your conduct, desires, plans, and overall life, it is possible you have not decided to commit your life to Christ fully. It is easy to become a lukewarm Christian without commitment and studying the Holy Scriptures for yourself. Stop right here and examine yourself and walk.

THE WAY AND PROCESS OF PURIFICATION

Again, God's attempt in transition is to get us to a special place in Him. The goal is first to get us through, then to. The process can be tedious because of our prideful nature and the worldly influences surrounding us every day. For the best outcome during change, our ears must be pressed against the gates of heaven to listen for instructions. We do not have the answers in a season of the unknown, nor do we know the way. At a time in my wilderness, I found the making of the tabernacle of Moses immensely helpful in remaining focused. The instructions were literal for Moses but more symbolic for believers today. God instructed Moses in Exodus 25:8 to make a sanctuary for Him to dwell in. God wanted to establish a meeting place where He would meet with His people. Moses had to listen to every detail to make the temple. There was no way Moses could have done this on his own or in his own strength. Moses surely did not see the big picture of how significant the temple would be then and in the future. He had to rely on God for every single detail.

Remember that Moses and the Israelites were still in the wilderness during this time, meaning they were still in the transition phase, an unknown place. God had been faithful, leading them by a cloud by day and a pillar of fire by night (Exodus 13:21-22). He never left them unattended. He remained with them despite their fickleness.

Eight parts of the tabernacle would lead the priest into a sacred place with the Spirit of God. Each step is symbolic of how we should prepare ourselves to approach God's throne.

The ***Outer Gate*** found in Exodus 27:9-21 is where the access point is located. This is the door to the inner court. There was only one entrance to the inner court of the tabernacle. Today, Christ is the door to salvation (Romans 10:9-10), and He is the access point to the Father in heaven (John 14:6). This part was also located in the wilderness, which symbolizes the world and everything outside of the things of God, and all are welcome to enter this way.

The ***Altar of Sacrifices (Brazen Altar)***, found in Exodus 27:1-8, is the foretelling of the coming of Jesus Christ. An altar was built for the slaughtering of an animal to atone for the sins of Israel. This would be how to maintain their relationship with God when they sin. The altar represents restoration, maintaining and establishing a sacred order in the kingdom. This is Jesus Christ today. Isaiah prophesied His coming in Isaiah 53:5-8. Christ was the ultimate sacrifice in the process of purification (Matthew 27:32-56). We no longer need dead sacrifices to atone for our sins, but we have mercy through the living Christ.

The ***Bronze Laver*** is found in Exodus 30:17-21. The laver is a bowl or a pan of water. This is where the priest washed their hands and feet in the water. The water represents a cleanse. Before they could enter the meeting place with the Spirit of God or even go near it, they had to cleanse themselves with water. Today, this is symbolic of the spiritual baptism or water baptism (1 Peter 3:21). This process clears our consciences from our worldly nature and moves us closer to God.

The ***Holy Place (Inner Court)*** is found in Ezekiel 8:3,16. After the spiritual baptism, it is time to enter an intimate relationship with God. An inner court is a place of familiarity, closeness, affectionate or deep knowledge of another. Here is where we are transformed in life and experience the fullness of His presence and power. Your eyes will become open to greater insight and more wisdom by this time. It is essential to avoid any distractions at all costs because a wilderness season will offer more of one thing and less of something else, causing us to turn our backs on God like Israel did standing right in the inner court (Ezekiel 8:16).

The ***Holy of Holies (The Art of the Covenant)*** is found in Exodus 25:10-22. Once we've decided to transition from the world and into the gate of salvation, offered ourselves a living sacrifice at the altar, and been washed by the baptism of the Holy Spirit from all worldly conduct at the bronze laver, He welcomes us to come deeper with Him by entering an intimate relationship with Him. Now we are invited to enter the meeting place with God. The Holy of Holies is the mercy seat. This is where our sins are atoned, we are renewed, convinced, and we gain confidence in God.

Before the ark, there was the ***Gold Lampstand (Menorah)*** found in Exodus 25:31-40. The lamp represents guidance and is a type-shadow of Jesus Christ as He is the way, the truth, and the life (John 14:6). As a lamp guides us in a dark room, Christ guides us through life.

The ***Table of the Showbread*** is found in Exodus 25:23-30. The showbread was for the priest to eat when in the presence of God. Today this is symbolic of God's providence for the believer. This bread is also an act or lesson of thanksgiving. Every day, we should thank God for always providing for us daily.

And then there is the ***Altar of Incense*** found in Exodus 30:1-10. The incense burned day and night, and the smell would rise to God as He took pleasure in the sweet fragrance (Exodus 29:25). Today the incense is a symbol of prayer. Prayer should never stop once we have entered a place of holiness with the Father. It is in the holy place when your prayer life is developed, worshipping God in an upward position, lifting our voices to Him as we look to the heavens. We must stay renewed and refreshed to maintain this sacred place, but God is merciful that when we fall, we can repeat this process and begin again with Him.

THE CROSS AND THE UNVEILING

On February 11, 2021, I had just started a 21-day fast, and on this day, it was day four. I had a dream about two men talking about the veil of Moses. I was so intrigued that I vividly remember their conversation when I woke up. I knew God wanted to speak to me concerning a matter. In Exodus 34:29-35, Moses went up to Mount Sinai to commune with God, but this time God gave him the laws on two tablets. When Moses came down from the mountain top and appeared before Israel and his servants, verse 29 says, "His face was shone," meaning 'shine.' Moses had an unexplainable glow about him that he did not know he had, and it really creeped Israel out that they could not look at him. Why? Because they did not understand the nature of his glow. As I mentioned before, we tend to reject what we do not understand and are not open to understanding it.

We must not assume the presence of God does not permeate this way today. If you know of prayer warriors or prophets who understand that their office requires spending an immense amount of time in the presence of God, when you look at them, you see this inevitable glow. This is how you know when a believer has been in the presence of God. People are drawn to this glow, and some are blind to it or simply refuse to acknowledge it. It is even commonplace that people will also be intimidated, afraid, or jealous of the light that so evidently shines on you because they do not understand it or are unsure how to obtain it. In Israel's case, they were afraid of Moses. He looked different than before he went up to the mountain, and they did not know what to think about him or God. They could not explain his face in their own knowledge, so their pride led them to believe that something was wrong with Moses and because of Israel's position, Moses made a veil to cover his face when he addressed them, but when he was summoned to go up to the mountain by God, he would remove the veil. Moses allowed himself to be consumed by the fear of the people. He hid the glory of God from them. Have you been a Moses amongst your family, workplace, girl's night out, or even in church? So many believers are going about with the same veil Moses had to cover the glory of God.

For the same reason, fear of what others may think or say, it is preferred to accommodate the people instead of revealing God in your life. People hide the call/office to escape the controversy of being a follower of Christ. When we hide or so-called veil ourselves, it represents a hideaway, pride, and limitations. And when reaching such a place, it takes God to aid us and get us out of our comfort zone. By doing so, He will use a plague of any form or fashion.

It is safe to say that during crises leading to loss and destruction are not as bad as they appear to be. God simply uses cataphoric events to remove and replace. He removes any form of limitations and replaces them with freedom, increase, permission, and openness. We have found such commonality with the world that often, we do not realize we need liberation. God will provide this in a crisis or a season of change.

In the dream, I heard one of the men talking about the unveiling of Moses. I remember the man was so fascinated about the process of going beyond the veil. He was so exuberated as he talked to the other man, as I remember it. Moses' unveiling was only in the face of God. It is unfortunate that Israel was not able to bask in the glory that rested on his face. The unveiling of God's glory did not take place until the cross at Calvary, when Jesus committed the greatest and ultimate sacrifice for all humankind. He unveiled the glory of the new covenant. A covenant that would no longer penalize the fall of man to death but instead extend grace and mercy, granting a pardon for sin, and when we receive God's mercy, we humbly acknowledge our wrong. There is no room for pride in the humble. Through grace, we must understand that we receive what we do not deserve, and through mercy, we do not get what we deserve. The cross represented the worst kind of crisis that is hard to behold as we read about it or see with our imagination.

The mask we are required to wear due to COVID-19 is quite parallel to the mask many believers wear in the silence of being a believer of Christ, like the veil Moses wore in front of Israel. The death and resurrection of Jesus Christ give life through the Holy Spirit, which the laws could not give—making the new covenant much more glorious and effective. With that, under the new covenant of Christ, we have been granted a boldness to walk in and not live in the shadows of fear, shame, or intimidation. In 2 Corinthians 3:12-13, Paul urges believers not to mirror Moses wearing a veil over his face, hiding God's glory from others, preventing them from seeing His beauty, but to live in confidence given to us through the resurrection of Christ. In verse 14, he mentioned the hardened minds of Israel that from that day until now, at the reading of the Old Testament, the minds are still veiled, prohibiting the truth of the new covenant from being embraced. God will use a crisis of any kind to remove limits or unveil our understanding of life, and we must yield to even the hardships in life to evolve to our next. It is time to go beyond the veil and walk in the liberty He died for me to obtain.

GOD'S MORAL COMPASS

"Direct your child onto the right path, and when they are older, they will not leave it" (Proverbs 22:6). God's word is authentic and has been proven to be dependable for ages. However, in the new world, it is becoming more watered down by man's interpretation while diluting the actions. The scripture above guides parents to properly raise children to get the best outcome in their lives. It encourages parents to teach children how to exemplify good conduct that will lead to making the right decisions that when they become older, they will continue in that way. This passage became one of the church's cliches that I do not believe were taught correctly so we could see the fruit of the scripture. For the most part, many believers presume this scripture was to raise children in church, teaching them the importance of paying tithes and offering, singing in a choir, or serving on an auxiliary. When they were finished serving, they had to sit on that pew or chair, and they had better not mumble a word, chew gum, or even fall asleep. Sit up straight and participate in the service. During my generation, we were taught to look the part and save face, which was the same conduct as most parents attending church regularly. However, there was no moral guide, which is why most children raised in the church failed in their lives outside of the church but were more successful. The lack of morality led young people to lose interest in anything pertaining to the church.

There is nothing wrong with teaching a child religious practice, but we cannot neglect to teach them God's way of love and other areas of life. And the way God loves is unconditional. He does not stop loving us when we fall short or go astray. He is the God of no variations; He will not change His mind towards us.

Our children can only model after what they see adults do. If we are partial in life or even towards God, they too will become partial in their life and towards God. I have heard teens say their parents were not the best role models, and they believe this to be the reason they turned to other things, substance abuse or bad relationships, to find a sense of belonging and comfort. Some parents do not possess the skills of decent morality; however, that should never be an excuse not to learn morals because if we are still breathing, we all can learn. It is never too late to develop character and good conduct. Morality starts at home, so the child knows how to behave in society and in school to prevent suspensions or worse.

Another pandemic in the USA is bad policing against Black people, which we have seen this same plague in our history. So now more than ever, it must be a greater priority to train children right before they leave home for good how to be respectful, listen, comply, love, and forgive. If our children are taught to make good choices in the community, we can avoid a small fraction of young Black people dying at the hands of the police and each other or prevention from going to detention centers and/or jail. Here in Milwaukee, the juvenile incarceration rate has increased rapidly in the last year because of bad behaviors in the community, i.e., stealing cars, home invasions, or robbery. This could only mean there are breakdowns in the homes where **standards, boundaries,** and **assertiveness** are not being taught. **Standards** are rules or principles. As parents, we are the authority figures over their lives; therefore, we give them expectations and teach them what quality is. **Boundaries** indicate limits, keeping anything out that does not match their expectations, which are fashioned after the parent. These bounds protect them from the contrary. **Assertiveness** gives them self-assurance and the confidence to refuse temptations when it sticks its head out of the ground. They are confident in their standards and boundaries, which no one can make them feel bad for having. If we are going to teach these attributes, we must also live by them. In the eyes of the youth, we must demonstrate what we teach and expect out of life, and then children can apply what they learned by what was taught and what they saw through you.

I learned the hard way with my first-born daughter. For the first five years of her life, she saw me serving the world through clubbing, drinking, swearing around, and even at her, being very careless with what she watched on TV and simply coming and going as I pleased. I gave my life to Christ when she was five, and I did not realize there was so much work I had to undo in her little brain. The first four years of a child's life are the most important as they are like sponges during that time, retaining everything that is placed before them as a way of life. Well, in her first four years, she got partially responsible me. In other words, though I was living

DISCIPLINE IN THE WILDERNESS

on my own, working a full-time job, I was still living a little haphazardly and lacking obvious principles of how to organize my life properly where it could show up in her life. After I gave birth to my second daughter, we found a church home to fellowship with, and I thought I could use church practices to erase all the foolishness my oldest daughter had to witness in her tender years. Well, that did not go so well. My oldest daughter eventually succumbed to worldly conduct, and what I thought I was training her to do around the church did not really hold. In fact, it was the most ineffective teaching I have witnessed in my days as a believer. While I was embracing my new life as a believer, there were behaviors I had to unlearn for me to lead by example before her. It was a ball of confusion for both of us, but we made it through with the help of the Spirit of God. The main morality He taught me was love and patience with the process. And today, I am still holding fast and teaching this morality to both my girls to have with themselves, each other, and others.

When I obtained my master's degree in Bible Studies, I journeyed through the entire Bible from Genesis to Revelation in four years. Studying both the Old and New Testament, I learned so much about the character and nature of God, how He responds to certain things, what makes Him angry and what pleases Him. I learned His main moral of life is **love**. In both the Old and New Testaments are commands to love the Lord your God with all your heart, soul, and mind (Matthew 22:37, Mark 12:30, Deuteronomy 6:5, 10:12, 30:60). This is what God was attempting to teach Israel before their captivity, during their captivity, and after their captivity. He was simply demonstrating His love for them. Their bad behaviors put them in captivity, so God used the horrible conditions in Egypt to turn their hearts to His love. Why? Because anytime we face hardship, the first thing we result to is calling on a savior. We all have different saviors, but we cleave to that savior for divine intervention or answers. God wanted to be Israel's savior, so He ordained a hardship. God was teaching Israel unconditional love as He continues to teach this same lesson to believers today. No one saw COVID-19 coming, and no one can really say if God specifically inflicted us with this plague, but one thing is for sure, God is the God of all flesh and creation, and there is nothing under the sun He is not aware of. Certainly, we know He knew this was coming, and it was a wonderful opportunity to get everyone's attention back to what really mattered. COVID-19 was an opportunity to call on the Savior for answers, learn of Him, receive Him, and believe that He is the Sovereign God. Love covers a multitude of sins (1 Peter 4:8), and the scripture urges us to keep loving in action towards one another as it saves souls.

CONCLUSION

"All we like sheep have gone astray; we have turned, everyone, to his own way, and the Lord has laid on Him the iniquity of us all" (Isaiah 53:6). We leave and go our own way when we do not understand or have the answers in seasons. No one likes calamity or adversity; however, it is unfortunate they both are unavoidable and can sometimes be necessary to build up one's faith in God. In fact, over time, people have denied the very existence of God because of calamity. I have heard desperate souls say, "If God was real, then why does He allow innocent children to be harmed," or "Why is there world hunger." "Where is this God," they say. Some even assume God is not real due to senseless crimes, infant mortality rate, racism, diseases, and poverty. Only the carnal (not spiritual) mind, a mind that has been enlightened to God, would think this way. Desperately waiting for the unknown God to save the world, we sit and wait, all the while having no faith in Him, knowing that He can. We forgot that Christ has already saved the world (John 12:44-50). Notice in John 12:44 that Jesus had to shout to the people to get His point across because He was speaking to a people who had no belief in Him and extraordinarily little belief in God. His message to them was, "I came to be a light and save the lost, not to judge you if you fail to listen to Me." He acknowledges to them that the world was dark, and it needed the light of hope. He was the hope. I love how Jesus takes the attention off Himself and on to the Father who sent Him. He expressed that His coming and works were because He believed in the commands of His Father in heaven, which leads to eternal life. Jesus did not come in His own strength and might. He did not come to do His own will, nor did He come with only faith in Himself, but He had faith in his Father and the plan God had for Him, which allowed Him to walk with such confidence. This is what we do not have today, which is why it is easy to doubt the existence of God. We do not have faith in His plans for us, so we choose our own path and hope God comes with us. So, if God has already saved the world through the coming of Christ to shine a light on the evil that rests in darkness, He has done His part, and the rest is up to you whether you will believe in salvation for your own life, shining a light on any evil in you or around you. If the entire world believed the way Christ believed and followed as He did, the evil we see today probably would not exist so evidently. God is not responsible for the evil in the heart of man, but man is responsible for his own evil. At any time, man can turn their heart away from evil and toward God; the light of His hope will shine in them. Evil comes from darkness, and God is the God of light.

Evil is taught and does not genetically exist, and if this is the case, as we learn evil, we can also unlearn it and practice good. Just as evil is taught, so can good be taught. If you are breathing, the opportunity to gain experience is still available for you to grow and thrive in a new world.

Our belief system has gone unchecked and has been for quite some time now. The belief system is what moves the hand of God. Any time we believe in something or someone, we keep it alive through conviction. This can be tricky because we do not have proof or evidence of someone or something regarding faith or belief. It is a more special attribute of hope that keeps us believing. When times are unquestionable, we hold fast to our beliefs that when uncertainties come, the belief system is strong enough to maintain what we believe in and have the confidence to continue without fear, murmuring, and complaining.

Unexpected change or calamity is hard to deal with when you least expect it. In times of shifting, the life we once knew so well becomes different, and God is no longer with us. These times are brought on or allowed by God to bring us back to a place of devotion with Him, sincere devotion. God's power is infinite. No one will ever be able to fully explain or comprehend it all at once, and in times passing, we have denied the true power of God in our lives and the churches because sinful natures have occupied us. The part of us that so comfortably rules God out of our decisions, the irrational side that takes over, so the power of God no longer works for us. And because our works have overly consumed us, here comes calamity, shifting us into an unknown place or adversity. God must wean out the flesh again in the body of Christ as a whole and individually as His creation to bring us back to a disciplined place with Him by any means necessary. If we go through it right, we realize that we learn more during these downtimes than when our self-will consumes us more.

The biggest lesson I learned transitioning into my wilderness season was keeping my heart close to the Spirit of Christ. It played a vital part in writing this manuscript and getting by during the unknown. It was hard, but I fought to stay focused only on what He wanted during my transition, leading me to listen well to the Spirit's counsel and instructions for my life. My belief system staggered at times, and I may have questioned it out of anger, but every day, I found my way back to hope that I could continue to trust God in every awakening moment without going ahead of Him. This increased hope and trust have led me to begin drafting books (this one being the first) and buying my first home during a drought, uncertain times, and difficulties. Surely, discipline played a big part in my outcome in training my mind to stay positive and hopeful every day.

A wilderness is simply transitioning from one place to another, and during the transition, we face obstacles and life occurrences that are hard to reckon with. It feels like being in limbo or starting all over with something, with so many unanswered questions that could leave anyone in disbelief and doubt. So much so that we leave our faith. We veer off our path because we begin to pursue life as it was, attempting to control the outcome and results of the season. Transition is hard; however, it is important to surrender to the process during such times. Surrender to wherever the season is trying to take you to. It will not be the same as before wherever it leads you, but things will be different. We must not attempt to control the outcome by holding on to what is passing away, and certainly, as we transition into the new season, never look back or desire to go to the way things used to be. Looking back only deprives us of what lies ahead, and what is ahead is far more promising than what we left.

My oldest sister was a big support in writing this manuscript. In the wilderness, she was my sounding board as I transitioned into the unknown. She saw me leave a place I had depended on for some time. My transition was on February 28, 2017. Five years later, I watched as she, too, was led into a wilderness season on the very same day as mine. February 28, 2022, she decided to align with God and leave her job after 20 years. Leading up to that day, I watched her silently wrestle with fear and doubt and the thought of going back to what made more sense. Every chance I had, I would encourage her to stay the course and trust God. In the beginning, she had no idea why she was compelled to leave, but as time passed, the path became clearer. She has decided to go back to school in business as she and her husband launch their first business. Our wilderness's sole purpose is to catapult us into our next if we remain in God for guidance.

God knows what's best for us, but He will not superimpose on us. We must welcome His best for our lives, and it is then when we are able to flow and function in the day-to-day and the new season.

REFERENCES

Chang, Lulu. "10 Safari Horror Stories That Will Chill You To The Bone." Insider, Insider, Inc, 20 September 2018, https://www.insider.com/safari-horror-stories-2018-9.

Dowdy, Naomi. "4 Keys to How God Brings Transition." Charisma Magazine, Charisma Media, 16 September 2013, https://www.charismamag.com/life/women/10173-4-keys-to-how-god-brings-transition 09/16/2013.

Evans, Tony. "The Importance of Fasting." The Alternative Radio Online, 23 July 2018, https://www.youtube.com/watch?v=jze9pnqbK9U

Idled. (2022). *Dictionary.com*. Retrieved from https://www.dictionary.com/browse/idle

Kingdom. (2022). *Dictionary.com*. Retrieved from https://www.dictionary.com/browse/kingdom

Mercy. (2022). *Dictionary.com*. Retrieved from https://www.dictionary.com/browse/mercy

Pew Research Center. "In U.S., Decline of Christianity Continues at Rapid Pace." 17 October 2019. https://www.pewresearch.org/religion/2019/10/17/in-u-s-decline-of-christianity-continues-at-rapid-pace/

Spurt. (2022). *Dictionary.com*. Retrieved from https://www.dictionary.com/browse/spurt

Tzu, Lao. Goodreads, Goodreads, Inc, 2022. https://www.goodreads.com/quotes/8203490-watch-your-thoughts-they-become-your-words-watch-your-words

Wilderness. (2022). *Dictionary.com*. Retrieved from https://www.dictionary.com/browse/wilderness